DISABILITY

PASTORING FOR LIFE

Theological Wisdom for Ministering Well

Jason Byassee, Series Editor

Aging: Growing Old in Church
by Will Willimon

Birth: The Mystery of Being Born
by James C. Howell

Friendship: The Heart of Being Human
by Victor Lee Austin

*Recovering: From Brokenness and Addiction to
Blessedness and Community*
by Aaron White

DISABILITY

LIVING INTO THE
DIVERSITY OF
CHRIST'S BODY

BRIAN BROCK

Baker Academic
a division of Baker Publishing Group
Grand Rapids, Michigan

Published by Baker Academic
a division of Baker Publishing Group
PO Box 6287, Grand Rapids, MI 49516-6287
www.bakeracademic.com

Library of Congress Cataloging-in-Publication Data
Names: Brock, Brian, 1970– author.
Title: Disability : living into the diversity of Christ's body / Brian Brock.
Description: Grand Rapids, Michigan : Baker Academic, a division of Baker Publishing Group, [2021] | Series: Pastoring for life: theological wisdom for ministering well | Includes index.
Identifiers: LCCN 2020042365 | ISBN 9781540962973 (paperback) | ISBN 9781540964212 (casebound).
Subjects: LCSH: Church work with people with disabilities. | People with disabilities—Religious life.
Classification: LCC BV4460 .B76 2021 | DDC 259/.44—dc23
LC record available at https://lccn.loc.gov/2020042365

Unless otherwise indicated, Scripture quotations are from THE HOLY BIBLE, NEW INTERNATIONAL VERSION®, NIV® Copyright © 1973, 1978, 1984, 2011 by Biblica, Inc.® Used by permission. All rights reserved worldwide.

Scripture quotations labeled CEB are from the Common English Bible. © Copyright 2011 by the Common English Bible. All rights reserved. Used by permission.

Scripture quotations labeled ESV are from The Holy Bible, English Standard Version® (ESV®), copyright © 2001 by Crossway, a publishing ministry of Good News Publishers. Used by permission. All rights reserved. ESV Text Edition: 2016

Scripture quotations labeled FT are from *The First Testament: A New Translation*, copyright © 2018 John Goldingay. Used by permission of InterVarsity Press. All rights reserved.

Scripture quotations labeled GW are from GOD'S WORD, a copyrighted work of God's Word to the Nations. Quotations are used by permission. Copyright © 1995 by God's Word to the Nations. All rights reserved.

Scripture quotations labeled Jerusalem Bible are from *The Jerusalem Bible* © 1966 by Darton Longman & Todd Ltd and Doubleday and Company Ltd.

Scripture quotations labeled KJV are from the King James Version of the Bible.

Scripture quotations labeled NASB are from the New American Standard Bible® (NASB), copyright © 1960, 1962, 1963, 1968, 1971, 1972, 1973, 1975, 1977, 1995 by The Lockman Foundation. Used by permission. www.Lockman.org.

Scripture quotations labeled NCV are from the New Century Version®. Copyright © 2005 by Thomas Nelson. Used by permission. All rights reserved.

Scripture quotations labeled NET are from NET Bible®, copyright © 1996–2016 by Biblical Studies Press, L.L.C. http://netbible.com. Used by permission. All rights reserved.

Scripture quotations labeled NKJV are from the New King James Version®. Copyright © 1982 by Thomas Nelson. Used by permission. All rights reserved.

Scripture quotations labeled NRSV are from the New Revised Standard Version of the Bible, copyright © 1989 National Council of the Churches of Christ in the United States of America. Used by permission. All rights reserved.

Quotations from Amy E. Jacober, *Redefining Perfect: The Interplay between Theology and Disability*, foreword by Nick Palermo (Eugene, OR: Cascade Books, 2017), are used by permission.

Quotations from Bethany McKinney Fox, *Disability and the Way of Jesus: Holistic Healing in the Gospels and the Church*, foreword by John Swinton (Downers Grove, IL: IVP Academic, 2019), are used by permission.

Quotations from Rachel Wright and Tim Wright, *Shattered: God's View through Life's Broken Windows* (Farnham: CWR, 2019), are used by permission.

21 22 23 24 25 26 27   7 6 5 4 3 2 1

For two Agneses.
Laura Agnes McFarland,
from whom I received the faith I hand on to
Agnes Sophia Rose Brock,
who had a magic finger before her dad

Contents

Series Preface

One of the great privileges of being a pastor is that people seek out your presence in some of life's most jarring transitions. They want to give thanks. Or cry out for help. They seek wisdom and think you may know where to find some. Above all, they long for God, even if they wouldn't know to put it that way. I remember phone calls that came in a rush of excitement, terror, and hope. "We had our baby!" "It looks like she is going to die." "I think I'm going to retire." "He's turning sixteen!" "We got our diagnosis." Sometimes the caller didn't know why they were calling their pastor. They just knew it was a good thing to do. They were right. I will always treasure the privilege of being in the room for some of life's most intense moments.

And, of course, we don't pastor only during intense times. No one can live at that decibel level all the time. We pastor in the ordinary, the mundane, the beautiful (or depressing!) day-by-day most of the time. Yet it is striking how often during those everyday moments our talk turns to the transitions of birth, death, illness, and the beginning and end of vocation. Pastors sometimes joke, or lament, that we are only called when people want to be "hatched, matched, or dispatched"—born or baptized, married, or eulogized. But those are moments we share with all humanity, and they are good moments in which to do gospel work. As an American, it feels perfectly natural to ask a couple how they met. But a South African friend told me he feels this is exceedingly intrusive! What I am really asking is how someone met God as they met the person to whom they have made lifelong promises. I am asking about transition and encounter—the tender places where the God of cross and resurrection meets us. And I am thinking about how to bear witness amid the transitions that are our lives. Pastors are the ones who get phone calls at these moments and have the joy, burden, or just plain old workaday job of showing up with oil for anointing, with prayers, to be a sign of the Holy Spirit's overshadowing goodness in all of our lives.

I am so proud of this series of books. The authors are remarkable, the scholarship first-rate, the prose readable—even elegant—and the claims made ambitious and then well defended. I am especially pleased because so often in the church we play small ball. We argue with one another over intramural matters while the world around us struggles, burns, ignores, or otherwise proceeds on its way. The problem is that the gospel of Jesus Christ isn't just for the renewal of the church. It's for the renewal of the cosmos—everything God bothered to create in the first place. God's gifts are not *for* God's people. They are *through* God's people, *for* everybody else. These authors write with wisdom, precision, insight, grace, and good humor. I so love the books that have resulted. May God use them to bring glory to God's name, grace to God's children, renewal to the church, and blessings to the world that God so loves and is dying to save.

Jason Byassee

Acknowledgments

Embarrassingly, very few academic theologians have engaged the disability experience in any detail. I am fortunate enough to work in one of the rare departments in the world where this is not true. I have several wonderful colleagues who work on these themes and with whom I can regularly discuss them.

John Swinton is a practical theologian who has had a sweeping influence on the field of disability theology. It has been a privilege to have him take me as a young scholar into the foreign land of disability theology. He has written a range of powerful books on mental illness and the pastoral questions that disability raises for churches.

Grant Macaskill is a New Testament scholar who over the last few years has been thinking increasingly intensively about autism and whose recent book I highly recommend (*Autism and the Church: Bible, Theology, and Community*).

Léon van Ommen is a practical theologian also thinking hard about autism and doing empirical research on L'Arche communities and autism-friendly churches around the world.

Having such colleagues means that I have the privilege of getting to know most of the people working in the field of theology and disability and that I am able to keep up to date with what is happening in churches around the world, disabled advocacy groups, and research networks on theology and disability.

To be a hub of excellence in an academic field also means that a fantastically rich and insightful group of students and fellow travelers become one's friends. This book was enriched by the preparatory conversations I had with Lorraine Williams, Lynsay Downs, Chantal Huinink, Kirsty Jones, and Bishop Anne Dyer; by the feedback on a draft from Paul Shrier and Jason Byassee; and by the Celtic Anglican bishops on whom I first tested out the squirm-inducing material from the first chapter during their retreat in Inverness in January 2020.

As I spoke about disability to Christians in various parts of the globe, I began to be aware that the incredibly rich and exciting discussion I was having with my colleagues and students had moved far beyond the ways of understanding disability that are common in the church today—and more importantly, what is *happening on the ground* in churches.

The time had come for me to speak plainly.

This book is an attempt to summarize in the simplest language I can the best of the insights we have discovered over a decade of thinking very hard about the disability experience and what it reveals about God, the world, and the church.

Introduction

Welcome. Gentleness. Presence. Attentiveness. Commitment. This is all Christians need to know about disability. Simple words that sometimes ask more of us than we want to give.

Most Christians have never thought much about disability. This little book is for Christians who want to know where to begin thinking about it. It offers support to Christians with disabilities who want to help other Christians be more welcoming to disabled people.

It is for pastors who are busy and care about ministry but don't have time to read a heavy academic book on disability.

It is for parents who have adopted or birthed a child with a disability and are amid the bewildering process of figuring out what this might mean for their view of God and their life in church.

It is for congregants who are painfully aware that there are people with various disabilities in their churches, whose lives can be a struggle, but are not sure how to extend a better welcome to them in church.

It is for Christians and their families who are struggling to understand how to relate to—and how God relates to—their loved one who has dementia or who has had a stroke or who has had a paralyzing accident.

Christians in all these positions are in a painful place but also one with great promise, because once we begin to think about disability, we find ourselves led into the heart of the gospel in incredibly fruitful ways. Thinking about the disability experience also reminds us that our lives are fragile and vulnerable and that our own disabling may concern us more directly than we had ever considered.

To begin to look directly at the diversity of the disability experience also promises to open our eyes to things in the Bible we had never before seen. In noticing the diversity of the bodily experiences of the people around us, we begin to glimpse aspects of Scripture that we had previously missed. To notice new details in the Bible is almost inevitably to be driven to revisit long-held theological assumptions about disability—and what it means to be a human being.

The aim of this book is to help contemporary Christians to take a journey. The journey begins by thinking about the *experience* of disability. Wrestling with what it might mean for each of us to become disabled offers readers a better vantage point from which to reconsider the unnoticed disability experiences in Scripture and the overlooked capacity of Christian doctrine to shed light on them. The aim of this journey is to help Christians reconceive how we live as church.

A lot of good things are said today in schools and governments and businesses about inclusion. Inclusion is good, but it still presumes that disabled people are a "they" whom "we" need to include. I want to help Christians get beyond this modern habit of assuming that we cannot talk about disability without dividing up humanity into those who have disabilities and those who do not. And I want to do it in a way that helps Christians reimagine the day-to-day activities of the church.

It is important to recognize that books that move directly to telling us how to act and live differently are ones that do not empower us to find our own ways to change. We don't need to be told what to do but shown how to think creatively about what needs to change in our churches.

The books that actually help us change begin by stimulating creative thought. Stimulating thought, however, very often entails melting down our certainties so that they can re-form in new shapes. Sometimes the only way to provoke and invite creative new insight is to produce confusion in place of misplaced certainties. Sometimes our ways of thinking are so shrunken and dried out that they need the uncomfortable process of roasting or scalding so that they can crack open and come to life again. This roasting and scalding is never comfortable. But it matters. Without spoiling the first chapter, let me urge you not to skip it—though it will be uncomfortable.

Once we see that something is wrong about our world, and our church, we can begin to respond to its inhuman and destructive aspects with real insight. Far too many Christians have never been caught on the horns of the dilemmas posed by the disability experience. The first chapter is designed to reveal the problem of disability for the church in all its complexity. It would be wrong to then immediately offer a formula for how to meet this dilemma.

Once the roasting is done, we have to tackle the job of rethinking how we once understood the disability experience. This is what we will work on in chapters 2, 3, and 4, which draw attention to the biblical threads and theological claims that can help us understand disability better. Having made this disorienting and reorienting journey puts us in the right place to receive some useful hints about how to move, practically, toward being a more welcoming church to all the diversity of humankind. We are in the right place because we will have both the tools to think creatively about the challenges of our own unique situations and a sense of where to look to begin to put these effective but practical hints into practice.

As we proceed, I will point in passing at other things interested readers might like to read among the more recent academic work in disability theology. The main way I will do this is by quoting the sources that have formed my thinking on a given topic.

Make no mistake, my final target is wholly practical. I want to help the church rediscover the power of a gospel that bubbles up in the interactions that the Holy Spirit is calling Christians into with those who today carry the label "disabled."

ONE

Nobody with Disabilities in Our Church

By chance or by providence, I officially entered middle age while preparing to write this book. The rite of passage was a visit to the emergency room one Saturday morning. I'd finally managed the cliché of injuring myself with a power tool during a weekend do-it-yourself job around the house.

That sunny Saturday morning in November I had been cutting up bits of old furniture and scrap wood for kindling with a circular saw. Next thing you know, I was cutting my finger. For a millisecond I felt nothing. "Whew!" I thought. "None of me is on the ground, really dodged a bullet there!" Then came the blood.

From the instant I saw it beginning to pool dark and red through the tattered gash of my yellow work gloves, my world began to tilt. First a little. Then a lot.

If I was angry at myself when I did it, I felt *really* embarrassed sitting in the emergency room with the other middle-aged guys with hands and arms wrapped in bloody bandages. Turns out that I had managed to sever the tendon on the back of my right middle finger.

I saw all my middle-aged friends again, along with a few new ones, over the next few months as I attended appointments for reconstructive surgery, follow-up care, and physical therapy.

In a flash, with a second's lapse of attention, my world had changed, radically unsettled. I'm right-handed. It's been months now that I've been *trying* to write this book with that mangled middle finger. It's been getting in the way, not just in my body but in my mind. I am amazed how the loss of a tiny portion of my flesh has so directly affected my capacity to *do* things. Even more shocking is how quickly and deeply not being able to *do* something alienated me from my familiar relationship with the world.

The finger is no longer transparent to my purposes. What I formerly could do without even thinking about my finger I can now sometimes not do at all. Other times I have to think far too much about how I am going to circumvent that darn finger, which not only doesn't work but is sticking out and getting in my way!

More unsettlingly, the loss of capacity has made me begin to worry about my identity. If I'm anything, I think of myself as a writer. I constantly need this finger to type or write longhand. How will I get on if it no longer works?

Only months later does it occur to me that the existential tremors that my damaged finger has unleashed in me might be a sort of gift. The finger has forced me to stop and consider what we're actually saying when we say that someone "is" disabled or "has" a disability.

I am not suggesting that my injury is equivalent to more serious or lifelong disabling conditions. I am grateful that it did not become infected, which could have been life threatening or even led to the amputation of the hand or more. What the injury has done is to help me think more concretely and to listen more closely and comprehend more of what people are really saying when they speak of disability experiences. One of the most difficult aspects of talking about disability is the awkward fact that most people have precious little first-hand experience of it—or think that they don't (more on this later).

Pastors and the Disability Experience

Most Christians today tend to think of disabled people as a class of people with serious physical, sensory, or mental impairments. Good people will extend kindness and a helping hand to them.

Unless it strikes someone close to them, the great majority of churchgoers tend not to think too often, or theologically, about disability in the church. Not having many chances to rub shoulders with those with disabilities, disability never seems to warrant close thought.

These assumptions explain many pastors' first response to the question of how they think about ministry to people with disabilities. Hans Reinders reflects on the most common way pastors speak about disability in their churches: "The times that I have asked ministers and pastors about members of their congregations who are disabled, the most frequent response is, 'We don't have them.'"[1] This is a remarkable claim. If it is true that most congregations do not have disabled members, huge numbers of people are not in church. If it is false, ministers are widely affected by the serious problem of not seeing what is in front of them. Either way, serious questions need to be asked about why this is such a common response among pastors when asked about disability.

Having little or no regular contact with people with special needs, most Christian pastors are therefore only slightly embarrassed to admit that they haven't thought hard, or theologically, about disability. They are not thinking about it because they are not regularly confronted with it in their church.[2]

Bethany Fox interviewed pastors from a wide range of Christian traditions in the Los Angeles area. Aside from pastors explicitly responsible for special needs ministries, she found most pastors tended to describe their relationship to people with special needs as "responsive." This is the second most common response from pastors when asked how they might relate to people who would come to their church with special needs. In one pastor's words, "When people come to us, then we try to answer those needs and help them in whatever way we can."[3]

Some pastors, Fox found, were able to remember having children with intellectual or developmental disabilities in their churches at one time or another. Few, however, could call to mind disabled people who were currently in their churches. Somehow, disabled people seemed to disappear from church after passing Sunday school age—despite the fact that mentally, they still *were* Sunday school age.

The stories pastors told about those with special needs in their congregations were almost always framed in terms of the needs for help or accommodation that those people brought into the congregation.

It seems clear that most pastors perceive the appearance of someone with disabilities in church as a challenge. They create "burdens and practical tasks for the church's leadership that benefit only the people with disabilities themselves."[4] These are the facts on the ground about pastors' views of what it means to have people with special needs in church. The question is why these views are so widespread and powerful. On closer examination, we discover that they are deformations of the Christian gospel that affect far more than pastors.

Where Are People with Special Needs on Sundays?

The United Kingdom is home to about sixty-six million people. Official government statistics calculate that over eleven million of them have a limiting long-term illness, impairment, or disability. The most commonly reported impairments are those that affect mobility, lifting, or carrying. This hints at why the prevalence of disability rises with age. Around 6 percent of children are disabled, compared to 19 percent of working-age adults and 45 percent of adults over state pension age.[5] About 13 percent of the population of the United States live with a disability, according to government statistics.[6]

There are clearly many people around with disabilities. Yet people with disabilities are statistically far less likely to attend worship services, Bible studies, and other church activities than those without disabilities.[7] How can this be? Could people with disabilities need God less? Perhaps they don't want to worship with other Christians?

Far from it.

One recent US study of more than four hundred churchgoing families with a special needs child found that a third had left a church because they found it unwelcoming. Almost half said that they had refrained from participating in some church activity because they felt their family member was not welcome.[8]

Erik Carter is a social scientist who focuses on the question of what makes a church, synagogue, or mosque successful in welcoming people and families with disabilities. In a large empirical study undertaken in the US, he found that the common denominators expressed by people with disabilities are that they wanted to be present, to be invited, and to be welcomed and known as well as accepted, supported, cared for, needed, and loved. He also discovered that churches trying to meet these aims in the standard way—through inclusion—have problems reaching these goals. As Carter observes,

> Contemporary conversations about inclusion in churches tend to be limited in two ways. First, they frame inclusion as a construct primarily concerned with physical location. Such a narrow lens neglects the primacy of relationships, which can still be limited or altogether absent even when people with and without disabilities navigate the same spaces. Second, they do not place the personal perspectives of people with disabilities and their families at the forefront of the discussions. Such an omission can inadvertently lead congregations to adopt practices that ultimately do not lead people to feel welcomed and valued.[9]

Amy Jacober is a theology professor with over two decades of on-the-ground experience in various capacities with the parachurch organization Young Life Capernaum. Young Life Capernaum hosts weekly events and annual summer camps to share the gospel with and disciple teenagers with disabilities. Jacober has also done extensive surveys of the experiences of children, teens, and families in churches. In her interviews, she asked the neutrally worded open-ended question, What is your experience with church? What she found agreed with other research showing that people with disabilities (and their families) very often experience church as an unwelcoming environment.

> Overwhelmingly, the experiences were negative. . . . One mother offered this response, "So I tried to look and every church I called, I asked 'is there a place for a special needs child?' every year as he got older—ten, eleven—there was not one church that I found that had a place for special needs kids. . . . I could not believe with all of the programs we have . . . there's nothing that would have a child with disabilities and stay connected and get taught about Jesus or anything spiritual." Again and again I was told that families cherished the church, but once they had a child with a special need, they could no longer be involved. I heard stories of being asked to leave as their child was too disruptive. Others were told that no one was able to handle their child. For many, they experienced sitting in pews, working hard

to "handle" their own child and no one came to say hello, let alone help. What all but a few had in common is that they felt unwelcomed in countless small ways. It wasn't that anyone told them out loud church was no place for a family impacted by disability, but that was the message they received loud and clear. At some point, they just got too tired to keep trying and experience rejection and stress in a place that was established by God to allow us to bear one another's burdens.[10]

In radiating this passive lack of welcome, churches, like most places in modern Western societies, become yet another social space into which people with special needs feel they can't go. The reasons these social domains are experienced as no-go zones are pretty obvious, as one leader in disability studies joked: "People with disabilities were a cultural minority because they, like other minorities, shared a cultural diet: fast-food drive-throughs. Drive-throughs sidestepped the difficulties of physical and social barriers. Eating and living in private—due to physical and stigmatizing barriers—has defined what it has meant to be disabled."[11] This observation is particularly painful to Christians, since the church's self-understanding is fundamentally rooted in the idea of being open and welcoming to every human being. Christians like to think of themselves as more welcoming than McDonalds.

Ironically, those who work to give adults with intellectual disabilities a meaningful life are always on the lookout for free activities to which they can take those in their care to give them the chance to mix with, and perhaps even find friends among, the full diversity of the wider public. Activities they can do without paying to join in are incredibly difficult to find.

How often do those in group homes come to our churches?

On Failing to See

The demographic data seems to confirm many pastors' sense that people with special needs, especially those with learning difficulties, are not in church. The "we don't have any" view of pastors looks suspiciously like a self-fulfilling prophecy. The aim of this opening chapter is to examine the psychologically powerful assumptions that perpetuate this self-reinforcing prophecy.

We need to understand why disability lives in the outer reaches of most Christians' consciousness. When disability is assumed to be a marginal human experience, it can only become a conscious topic for pastoral or theological reflection when it befalls a family member or loved one. If we skip asking *why* Christians don't recognize the disabilities of their neighbors as theologically and pastorally significant, we will have little ground to explore the biblical and theological issues that it raises.

It would be saying too much to assert that without discussing experience we cannot read Scripture rightly. But when Christians have considered disability not worth the effort to think well about, they will be forced to cobble together answers to the questions it raises under the pressure of a pastoral dilemma. We can do better. Answers cobbled together under pressure are rarely well thought out.

Here's the amazing truth: once we begin to give a little more concerted effort to thinking well about the disability experience, we discover that what we once experienced as a threatening disability crisis now appears as a promising gateway to a truly life-giving way of following Christ.

The Disabling Experience

I opened with the story of my finger to highlight why the experience of being able-bodied makes it so difficult to take disability seriously as a theme deserving more concerted attention from pastors, theologians, and church people.

My disability experience begins with a finger. Yours might begin with your eyes, your ears, your back, your knees, or even your memory. You will no doubt have already begun to come into contact with disability secondhand as someone you know has mental health issues, a birth defect, or a learning difficulty.

Probably the first thing I learned from my finger injury was how quickly worries arise—and how all-consuming these worries are—about what will happen if the loss of function is permanent. The second realization comes hot on the heels of the first one—you discover how shockingly distorting intense or chronic pain is on the mind, how disorienting it is. As the pain subsides, one begins to learn how many formerly easy things have become difficult or impossible with one hand—washing your hands, for instance, or carrying an object of any size while trying to open a door, or pulling a trash bag out of a can.

Perhaps for the first time in my life I was experiencing disability firsthand. I had been literally dis-abled. I had been rendered unable to *do* things I had once done without a second thought. The finger, once so useful to me, now constantly gets in the way, bumping into things and making it almost impossible to write.

The injury happened the week before I was to take an international trip. The surgeon told me that it would probably be best to leave the bandages in place for the nearly three weeks of the trip rather than trying to change them on my own while traveling.

The trip was to California, where I had to lecture and go to conferences through the most painful and awkward phase of the recovery process. Often, I had to elevate the hand in order to keep it from pounding with pain. The trip fell just before Thanksgiving. I spent this one as a guest at a pastor's house with several congregants from around the world, including an elderly bishop from an African American Pentecostal tradition.

I'd been to healing services before, but I'd never been cold called for a body part to be grasped and prayed over. At first, I wasn't sure what was going on. It clicked in when I heard the line, "We pray for the enemy spirits to come out."

Having my hand grabbed and prayed over certainly surprised me, though I did not find it offensive. It was not too different from shaking hands, after all. It was, however, my first personal experience of being "ambush healed." For the first time I directly considered how uncomfortable it would be to have the preacher's hands over my ears if I were deaf or, as some have experienced, to have their unseeing eyes anointed with the preacher's spittle (following Jesus's example in Mark 8:23; John 9:6).[12]

About a week later, back in Scotland, a friendly nurse gently unwraps the finger I've not seen in weeks. As the bandages come off, I am shocked.

Disability as Shocking

The finger looks revolting, in the technical sense of the term—it makes my stomach turn. It looks nothing like it used to. Purple, swollen. The skin broken and mottled, and an angry gash and open wound across the knuckle. I am repulsed. This is not "me." I'd almost rather it be gone. To the nurse, however, the finger is just another body part needing attention. She soaks and scrubs and peels dead skin and picks out stitches. I have to admit it looks a little better. I'm grateful, but boy does the finger still feel odd.

It is odd to say, but in the weeks it has been wrapped up it has somehow become an "object" to me. It has transformed into a stiff, painful, and ugly thing, something that I don't use but instead work around and try not to think about. What was once one of my most useful bits of flesh first became an object, then a problem to be fixed, "a project."

My mind whirls with the implications of my ugly metamorphosis. My actual body now challenges my subconscious assumptions about the "beautiful finger" that I never realized I had. (Here the mind boggles. How must the paraplegic feel after an accident that has left their whole body uncontrollable and a barrier to doing what they would like to? How must someone who has been badly burned feel about the pain and disfigurement of their new bodily form?)

Even as my finger heals, its incremental improvements do not reconcile it to me. It stiffens, it is discolored, the nail is lumpy and misshapen—nothing like its twin on my left hand.

I've been talking about my personal, subjective experience, but it is important that we pause and sit with this reaction for a moment. What does it mean to experience a part of our *own* bodies as revolting, repellant? First, a part we once related to as likable and functional has been *alienated*. I no longer immediately experience it as "me" because it now feels to me like an "other." It does not do what I ask it to and instead actively obstructs my goals by sticking out there and constantly getting in my way.

Second, alongside this practical difficulty comes a strange aesthetic reaction. I simply don't like the way it *looks*. My own body is dragging me one finger at a time into new categories, categories that Christians do not easily admit they have: between working and useless bodies; between beautiful and unsightly bodies.

My being repelled by my finger is thus a sign of an old, old problem, long ago recognized by the early church. Even when we are not aware of it, we harbor unacknowledged images of beautiful and likable bodies. Body *images* so deeply shape our own aspirations and self-understandings that they almost inevitably color our views of other people's bodies, making it difficult for us to love them.

If we are able to be disgusted by a *part of us* that we once loved as ourselves, how easily will we justify our desire to escape from making eye contact with the burn victim or the person with some other disfigurement? Their unsightliness first repels us and then makes it easy for us to justify our lack of love.

We don't see disabled people around us because we have images of useful and beautiful bodies and attractive minds to which they do not conform. It is easier not to look at them, because if we give them our attention, it makes us anxious.

Disability as Identity Challenging

For a while (several months, in fact) I had to wear a splint to immobilize the most affected joint in my wayward finger in order to protect the surgically repaired tendon from detaching. The splint rubs against the adjacent fingers, making the already stiff and unwieldy digit even more painful and awkward. To add insult to injury, the splint doesn't help me *do* anything. Its only promise is that it will help me regain function in the future—if I keep wearing it.

Immobilizing a joint causes muscles to contract and joints to stiffen at an alarming rate. Anyone with any sort of paralysis will know this better than I do.

I could not but think: What if I was struggling to gain mobility not in a finger but in a hand, not in a hand but in a whole arm, not in a single limb but in my whole body? What would it be like to not be able to control the muscles in my tongue or those that direct my eyes?

My stiffening finger is giving me new eyes for the stiffened knees of the person who has had ankle- or knee-replacement surgery. It is making me reconsider the experience of stiffened ankles and wrists of the person with cerebral palsy, as well as the awkwardness of the hands limited and drawn into immobility by other paralyzing conditions.

I'm genuinely unsure whether it will ever regain enough flexibility to curl my right hand around a pen. For someone who writes every day, sometimes for hours a day, this is not a superficial worry. The loss of this *particular* bodily functionality threatens my identity.

While I can still write, the hand that once transparently recorded my thoughts has become a cumbersome and awkward barrier to that very process. My body seems determined to upend "me"—or at least that "me" that I have put so much of myself into.

As it heals, the finger begins to recover function—laboriously and incompletely. As it does, I cannot but feel a pang of loss. I've not lost a whole finger, thank God, let alone a limb, but the function will never be the same. It will always hurt and be sore in the cold or if I hit it.

Thus in every waking hour my finger, in all its pain and awkwardness, continually poses a question to me. It holds before me a set of losses; it forces me to grapple with my body's ugliness; it unsettles the certainty that I know who I am.

Ultimately the questions it presses on me are more basic: Will I embrace or fight the alteration of self-image this entails? Is this new unsightliness and unwieldiness really who I am? These are questions that will not be answered without squarely facing how my finger now deviates from my unconsciously embraced ideals and dreams of aesthetic and functional normalcy.

Put theologically, can I really accept my *own* unsightly member? As we have seen, this is a theological question because my own bodily ideals are tied up with how I think of the worth of others' bodies. My finger raises the question: Do I *truly* accept those in the body of Christ who diverge from my ideals? The aesthetic and functional ideals I must confront if I am to accept my finger are not ones Christians can typically admit. Unacknowledged ideals die hardest.

Theologian Frances Young's son, Arthur, has cerebral palsy. It is worth pausing to define cerebral palsy, since we will meet several people in chapters to come with this medical diagnosis. Cerebral palsy is an umbrella term for a condition springing from damage to the brain that usually occurs in the womb. The damage to the brain may cause epileptic seizures, and it is often associated with difficulties in controlling the muscles. This lack of muscular control often causes sight and communication difficulties, as well as the contraction of large muscles, which can be quite painful. In more severe cases it can also cause learning difficulties. Arthur's cerebral palsy is quite substantial, and he was never able to walk or talk.

Young had raised Arthur to adulthood when she visited a L'Arche community in France. L'Arche is a global movement in which Christians with and without learning impairments live together. At one meal Frances found herself sitting opposite Edith who, like Arthur, had cerebral palsy. She writes, "To my shame, I felt disgusted by her slobbering her food, the red wine she clearly loved splattered all over the napkin round her neck. I was deeply chastened by my reaction—perhaps I was meant to see how people sometimes felt at table with my son."[13] Frances's bracing honesty takes us to the point of no return in this first chapter. We will get no further if we refuse to admit the disgust, resistance, or discomfort some people evoke in us.

My finger offers me the gateway to a true understanding of disability precisely in its defection from my ideals about what I want it to be. The truth is that I don't like what has happened to me, I don't like how my finger looks or how it works, and if I could bring the old finger back, I certainly would. This is a defining spiritual moment. I can choose to hide from these negative feelings, to bury my loathing of my body part and pretend that I don't feel it. If I take this route, however, I will have to build up defenses against the questions of others about my finger. I will also have to deny or suppress my anger at what I feel I have lost in its ugly metamorphosis.

There is another road. I might admit my vulnerability and discomfort. I might squarely face the challenge to my self-identity my body is forcing on me. Down this road lies transformation.

We've all met elderly people who cannot reconcile themselves to the aging of their body or to the loss of the capacity to drive or live by themselves. Often such refusals to accept loss render elderly people increasingly frustrated and angry. Some of us may have met a pastor or another person with a degenerative disease who refuses to let it be spoken of openly and reacts aggressively to any suggestion that the time might have come to consider letting go of some duties.

The apostle Paul wrote to the Corinthian church: "Those parts of the body that seem to be weaker are indispensable, and the parts that we think are less honorable we treat with special honor. And the parts that are unpresentable are treated with special modesty, while our presentable parts need no special treatment" (1 Cor. 12:22–24). Do we have any idea what this really means?

Breaking Disability Down

At the most basic level, my finger injury resulted in what is called an *acquired* disability. It was not a *congenital* disability, one I was born with. From the beginning the surgeon reassured me that the severed tendon would heal in time, and I would regain full functionality. That means mine would be a *temporary* disability. The acute phase of my ordeal lasted about three months. Yet it was an ordeal, a condition that would pass in one way or another. It was not a *permanently* disabling condition, even if it had some permanently function-reducing effects.

The disabilities that come into most people's minds when they hear the term "disability" are importantly different from mine. When people hear the word "disability," they think of people who are totally blind or deaf, are in a wheelchair, or have visible conditions such as Down syndrome. The iconic conditions that come to mind when people think of a "disabled person" are only the tip of the iceberg.

Of course, many conditions fit fairly easily with this common imagination of disability: locked-in syndrome, cerebral palsy, and Tay-Sachs disease, to take a few examples. Even these unambiguous cases, however, may have come into people's lives in very different ways. The same bodily or mental disability may thus raise remarkably diverse pastoral questions.

There are congenital disabilities that exist because a pregnant mother came into contact with an infection from a cat during pregnancy. Other congenital conditions may come from fetal alcohol syndrome or contact with environmental toxins. The different effects on pregnancies can produce a wide range of birth anomalies, including missing or extra limbs, missing or extra digits, or conjoined twins or twins where one has been negatively affected in the womb.

All these disabilities fit comfortably with the popular imagination of disability. But for some conditions, it is much less clear whether the condition is a disability. While certain conditions may be visible, the condition's power to stigmatize a person is more important than the minimal loss of functionality, such as misaligned eyes or a stutter. In such cases labeling the condition a disability may cause offense to people who do not wish to be singled out for their condition.

Also at the margins of the popular imagination of disability are those people who most assume have obvious functional deficits but who resist being labeled "disabled," such as Deaf or autistic people. Many in both groups are happy to be called Deaf or autistic but *not* disabled.

Some people who wear medical labels of disability have received that label because of their inability to do some things, even though this inability is not immediately visible, such as those with epilepsy, general anxiety disorder, or chronic pain. For them the label "disability" may be crucial for getting the treatment they need even if many people would not recognize them as disabled and they might prefer that other people not know about their disability.

Taking a close look at these different experiences of disability highlights the reality that there is no *one* thing called disability, no *single* disability experience. In fact, in a way few terms are, the term "disability" is an artificial category, a category that does not obviously refer to a single thing. This does not mean that the physical and mental conditions to which it refers are not real—far from it. It means only that the category is so wide and diverse that it can sometimes mislead more than it illuminates.

It can be compared with an artificial category like "things that are in books." Many things are talked about in books, practically anything you can think of. People put bookmarks and flowers between the pages of books. People write notes in books. Almost an infinity of things are "in books." So to say that something is "in a book" is not saying much. It is not denying that there are many things in books; it is just not telling us which things are meant.

So even though the term "disability" is not very precise, it is a term that is so widely used that Christians cannot, and indeed will not want to, avoid using it. We just need to use it thoughtfully. When Christians use the term "disability," the main trap to be avoided is thinking of "other people" as disabled. A close second is reducing people *to* their disabilities. The advantage of the language of disability is its breadth, its capacity to draw attention to a wide range of human diversity and life challenges. The best way not to let the language of disability trap us is to break it down into its constituent parts.

We also must avoid thinking of all disability as equivalent to *either* disease or injury. My finger was *injured*, but what resulted was a *temporary* disability. I had a *disability experience*, but I did not *become* disabled. I experienced a reduction of my capacity to do things, but, in the end, I did not come to identify myself as disabled. My temporary disablement could well have been formally recognized by my employer giving me a few weeks of sick leave. If I had injured a different part of my body, such as my leg or back, the government might have recognized my reduction of mobility by giving me a special parking permit, officially labeling me "disabled."

Breaking down the idea of "disability" to reveal the assumptions that support it helps us think Christianly because it teases apart assumptions about disabled people that commonly lump different types of disability experience together. It helps us appreciate the genuine, and important, differences between human experiences. It has also highlighted the fluid boundary between what we commonly assume to be "normal" and the disability experience. Breaking disability down raises the question of whether the term "normal," which is its linguistic opposite, deserves the same treatment.

Escape from the Norm

The term "disability" functions more like a mean, in the mathematical sense. If we take one hundred numbers, some are nearer to the outer limits of the set, and some are closer to the middle. The one at the very middle is the mean. If we change the numbers in a group, the mean changes.

The same goes for disability. It is a category that defines a shifting set of human experiences. By implication, what we think of as "normal" is really only the name we apply to that group who looks most like they lie nearest the center of all the human beings we've ever come across. The problem is that the numbers one and one hundred are not intrinsically inferior to the number fifty. But if fifty is taken as the norm, suddenly one and one hundred can be perceived as broken, as odd, as weird.

If we want to think Christianly about disability, it is crucial that we not import presumptions about what is "normal" that make us assume that those humans who are "rare" are problems, as natural as this habit may be. "Normal" is always an imagined entity. In earlier centuries theologians like Augustine imagined the norm using the categories of platonic philosophy, in which there was one perfect human form from which each actual human diverged more or less.

Today we think of the norm in statistical terms. What is normal is what most people are like.

We must learn to relinquish from the outset the assumption that most people are "normal." It is crucial to do so because when we think this way we cannot but assume that those who have a disability are by definition not "normal." Belief that some people are "normal" generates a basic problem of thinking that runs like this: "If most people have these kinds of bodies and minds, then they are normal/correct, original/healthy. And those whose bodies are different surely wish they were like the rest."

This is precisely the logic that made me repelled by my finger. My other nine fingers look and work in one way, but now one finger is different. I wish it were like the others. But it is not. In disability theology this is called the "normate assumption." I simply assume that the best way for a finger to be is like my other fingers. I never pause to think about the fact that I have one finger that is not like the others, and I will have to either accept this or psychologically repress my distaste for it. No matter which road I choose, my finger will never again be like the other fingers. I make a normate assumption when I think of my "normal" fingers as my "real" fingers. This assumption positions my one "damaged" and "unpresentable" finger as the one that will hold me back. This normate assumption stops me from receiving my one different finger as good, even though it remains functional in its own particular and unexpected way.

Grappling with the problems raised by the sheer diversity of the conditions lumped together under the single term "disability" highlights the first and most significant theological point to grasp when beginning to think about disability: getting disability right means *paying close attention to particularity*. I am going to have to find out what my finger will do. I am going to have to find out the sense in which my finger and my hand have a new kind of beauty as they are—scar, bent knuckle, stiffness, and all. Behind this acknowledgment I will need to wrestle with the reality that God has at least allowed it to be this way.

When we transfer this insight about my relation to my own body part to relations with other people, we are really saying something very simple. Paying close attention to particularity really only means *listening* to people. People do have different forms of body and mind. But this does not mean that difference, even if rare, is something that needs to be changed. In the end this will have deep implications for us as we negotiate the disability experience in our churches. There will be no single "solution" or "answer" to the ecclesial dilemmas and pastoral questions raised by the many types of life experiences today labeled disabilities.

Inabilities to Imagine

My finger injury was an ordeal. It was only a passage. Painful, worrying, and threatening permanent loss and disablement at the time, but still a passage. The intense experience passed, transmuted into a scar, some unpleasant memories, and a wonky digit. It receded to only a part of a larger life. It was a passage *in* my life, not *a life*. And this is the problem. I find it very difficult to imagine anything more serious, more permanent, more life changing.

People who are born with conditions that I could experience only by losing some of my capacities have a very different disability experience. Those born without any fingers at all, for instance, often live remarkably full lives and eventually forget that some might label their condition a disability.

We come here to one of the most difficult problems in the discussion of disability: the gulf that separates physical disabilities from intellectual disabilities and mental illnesses.

Those who read and write books can relatively easily imagine acquiring a physical disability. But the very fact that we read and write proves we do not have a (significant) intellectual disability. It is also to be expected that readers with specific disabilities will resonate with some discussions and find others foreign and difficult to imagine.

Many people with physical disabilities find it uncomfortable to be lumped together under the heading "disability" with those who have more severe intellectual disabilities. Paralympians, for instance, are often highly trained and as competitive as any other Olympian. They can find it discomforting to have their sport compared with the Special Olympics, in which many competitors have learning impairments. Similarly, Deaf people or people with visual impairments can be offended when they are treated as if they are learning impaired. There can be quite a lot at stake practically in such labeling. I have a friend in Aberdeen who spent the entirety of his elementary school years in a school for the learning impaired—even though he only had sight loss.

Churches are often attracted to the testimony of a person with a physical disability whose story fits comfortably within the narrative that Jesus has saved them and helped them to overcome adversity. But those who can't fit this script because they can't speak, because they haven't "won" or "succeeded" in life, or because they live with ongoing mental illness challenge this narrative of salvation as breeding success and performance. To recognize the problem here is to be invited to a much deeper understanding of the gospel.

Who is Jesus to people who cannot be a success in the terms we would like to achieve? Who is Jesus to those who are not "healed" from physical or mental conditions we would like to have removed if *we* suffered them?

Christians are often so busy wanting to be successful, to be part of growing and therefore desirable churches that *within the terms of our gospel* those who seem not to be able to achieve those objectives become a problem. This may be the central spiritual challenge facing contemporary Christians. People with autism highlight why this conflict about what the gospel means is the heart of the problem of disability for the church, as Grant Macaskill observes.

> Persons with autism are often treated with a form of contempt within the church, just as they are in wider society. Those whose autism is less

severe—who might have been diagnosed with Asperger syndrome until its removal from the diagnostic categories—are often dismissed as eccentric or are simply undervalued because they are less charismatic or "likeable" than others. They may be marginalized, may be the object of jokes, or may be seen as oddities. They do not conform to expectations; they do not fit in. Those with profound autism, meanwhile, will often exhibit disruptive behaviors that may well lead to exclusion, both for them and for their families. Churches and church leaders will often pray that their numbers will grow by God providing young families, and that their needs will be met by God providing wage earners and promising future leaders; they pray, in other words, for normal solutions to the challenges they face and expect divine blessings to have such normality. The presence of a socially challenged adult with a recent diagnosis of Asperger syndrome or of a disruptive child with profound autism will not necessarily be seen as an answer to such prayers.[14]

We find it almost impossible not to pity those who lack some capacity that we would be lost without—our sight or hearing, our capacity to speak or think. Our vision of people who seem not to possess one or more of these capacities is thus deeply skewed. We simply cannot imagine from where we are what their lives are like, because for us to get to their position would demand we *lose* capacities that we love and rely on.

But how would you experience your life if you had never *had* those capacities? Do we feel cheated that an eagle can see far better than the most well-sighted human? Are we embarrassed at our capacity to think just because there are people whose IQs qualify them to join Mensa?

We can envy those with greater capacities than us or pity those we suppose to have less. Yet it is worth noticing that those who tend to be most pitied, those with the most severe intellectual disabilities, are very often the ones most comfortable with who they are, at home in what they can or can't do.

The Gateway to Disability Theology

I can feel my finger and its pain and awkwardness. I can sense my feeling of repulsion at it. And I must look squarely at the sense of loss it evokes in me. I can also imagine how I would feel if it was my leg so that I could not walk or my eyes so that I could not see. I imagine the desolation I would feel if I were blind or deaf or quadriplegic.

Here is the problem: when I see someone else with one of those conditions, it is almost impossible to avoid projecting the desolation *I* would feel at such losses onto others who experience the condition totally differently. "Poor you," I reflexively think. "What a suffering to be like that." Projecting our fears and pity onto others who have disabilities we would prefer not to experience is totally normal—for sinners. It is not easily surmounted. We are at the gateway to doing disability theology the moment we decide to fight.

The simplest definition of disability theology is this: theological work necessary for us to receive with joy and practical welcome, and without sentimentality or pity, each and every human being as one for whom Christ died.

It is part of being a human to be unable to *do* things. It is part of *our* being human that we will not be able to *do* things. The condition of not being able to *do* what others can is today called "having a disability." Christians, however, do not know themselves or others in terms of what we or they can *do* but in terms of what God in Christ has *done for us*. We are the sort of creatures for whom God has professed love. This love is never withheld from us because of the capacities we may or may not have. God does not just love smart people. God does not just love people who can do lots of things.

After Frances Young's first feeling of disgust while sitting at a meal with Edith, whose cerebral palsy made her eating seem so unsightly, Frances gradually began to admit her feeling of repulsion and the pain it caused in relation to her own son. Admitting this disgust was the gateway to transformation:

> Sometime later, on another visit, I sat next to Edith on a sofa after the meal, gently trying to restrain her self-abuse as she repeatedly banged her head with her fist. . . . I'd been through the repulsion, I'd reached compassion—the wonderment was still to come. Next time I visited, Edith had just died. I joined the wake where person after person gave testimony to what Edith had meant to them—it challenged my French, but was somehow all the more powerful for being only half-understood. Afterwards a small group of us visitors went . . . to see Edith laid out

in the little chapel . . . , surrounded by flowers and candles, still and at peace, quite beautiful. We simply gazed in wonderment.[15]

"The parts that are unpresentable are treated with a special modesty," writes Paul, "while our presentable parts need no special treatment." The foundation of the Christian view of disability is contained in the next word: but. "But God has put the body together, giving greater honor to the parts that lacked it, so that there should be no division in the body, but that its parts should have equal concern for each other. If one part suffers, every part suffers with it; if one part is honored, every part rejoices with it" (1 Cor. 12:23–26).

Becoming One Body

To the extent that my finger made me incapable of being like everyone else and doing what everyone else could do, I was disabled by my injury. I discovered through it, however, a more unsettling truth. My injury and disability exposed my disgust at a member of my own body. My misshapen finger also revealed how easily I could be disgusted at others' bodies.

My injury was a trauma. When I recall the blood welling up through torn yellow gloves, the feeling of dread still rises unwanted in my stomach. I might think that the finger is ugly and want to say that it is somehow "not me"—but my body knows better, viscerally.

Not long after the injury I watched a popular gangster film that included a scene in which a gangster "sent a message" by throwing a grocer who had insulted his daughter to the ground in the street. He then stomped the grocer's hands on the edge of the curb for good measure.

The image again hit me straight in the gut. How could he wantonly inflict such horrific damage on a hand that would take months or years to heal and that would never be the same? My own disability experience had begun to do its work. I was beginning to glimpse what it might mean to genuinely "suffer with those who suffer." I was beginning to have an inkling of what it means to be a member of the body of Christ. It was a lesson that had to be learned against the grain of modern definitions of health and disability.

In the contemporary developed world our understanding of disability and healing is biomedical. We think of disability and healing in *mechanical* and *individualistic* terms. Mechanical, because we relate ourselves to other people in terms of what their bodies and minds can and cannot do. Individualistic, because we assume that a disability is a problem of the individual whose body is not "normal." In this way "biomedicine frames the conversation about what counts as something 'wrong' with an individual, and healing takes place when that 'wrong' is removed,"[16] as Fox observes. In the biomedical imagination, my finger is a classic instance of a disability in need of healing.

In the first Christian centuries, lepers, with their disfigured extremities, were the paradigmatic image of disabled outcasts. It was in wrestling with the disabled figure of the leper that the Christian church first began to hammer out its theology of disability. By taking on the challenge of the outcast and unsightly leper, these early Christians were asking what it means, concretely, that Jesus died to save every human being.

Yes, Paul admits, there are some in the Christian community who are different, whom we *think of* as weaker. *But the God of Jesus Christ clothes them in greater honor.* Paul immediately goes on to emphasize that because God clothes these ones who seem different in greater honor, a new social order emerges among Christians in which we are empathetically connected with one another. No cure in sight.

Christians follow a healing Jesus, absolutely. But the modern Christian expectation that Jesus's healing is simply about curing malfunctions in individuals' bodies is a truncated gospel. Jesus does change peoples' bodies by healing them. But he changes far more than bodies, as we will see in the next chapter. In changing their relationship to the eternal God, Jesus also changes their social status and their relationships to the religious authorities and their families.

The early Christians grasped the practical force of the biblical good news in rejecting the common, and humanly understandable, practice of shunning lepers as outcasts that was universal in the ancient world. Christians thus realized very early on that a church that cannot admit and root out its disgust at some bodies will not be a church that serves the reconciling and healing work of Jesus Christ.

The early Christians thought about disability because they realized that doing so is nothing more than thinking harder, deeper, and in a more rounded way about what it means to be a Christian.

The healing offered by Jesus Christ goes far beyond what modern mechanized and individualized pictures allow. It even goes beyond the responsivity that most pastors and congregants believe they extend to people with special needs. When Jesus's healing is afoot in a congregation, the surest sign that healing is happening is that the community is discovering creative, boundary-bursting ways to understand one another and live together as church.

The most likely reason why there are not more disabled people in our churches is that our unredeemed feelings and attitudes toward individuals with disabilities have somehow leaked out, through our looks and maybe even our actions, a message that people with disabilities are somehow not *really* welcome in our churches. To stop sending that message we must grasp—emotionally first and then intellectually—what it means to see one another as members of our own body.

This chapter has drawn attention to how critical it is for Christians to examine their own emotional reactions, especially our experiencing another person as unsightly, as unwieldy, as interruptive. The aim of this chapter has been to begin to think about disability where every Christian must, especially those who don't really feel like they know much about disability.

I began with a story about an injured finger to bring home the reality that living in a vulnerable, creaturely body means we are all one accident away from being disabled. And as we age, we are sure to become less able in one way or another. It is essential to start by attempting to get in touch with this truth at a visceral, emotional level if we are to have any hope of getting our theological thinking and practice in relation to disability straight. If we are still stuck in trying to ignore our own vulnerabilities, we will never relate truthfully to the vulnerability of others. The evasion of vulnerability is fatal to the church. It hurts disabled people directly, and this is a travesty. And as we will soon see, it also falsifies the life-giving gospel of Jesus.

My ultimate aim in this book is to convince you that being a church that has become comfortable welcoming people with all sorts of disabilities into church is just, well, being church. And that being this kind of church is genuinely exciting.

To get there I've tried to dislodge the extremely widespread idea that disability is only a problem sometimes, when someone shows up at church for whom we feel we have to make accommodations—perhaps because they cannot get up stairs or cannot hear or they make funny noises that we find distracting. When Christians think about disability as that kind of problem, they inevitably put it at the end of a very long queue of genuinely pressing problems—who is going to fix the leak in the roof, who is going to visit the shut-ins—the endless list of things that have to get done around churches.

Disability does not belong on that list. As long as Christians approach it in those terms, they will not be able to avoid sending out unwelcoming signals to people with disabilities in their churches. The problem of disability is really the problem of Christians negotiating their sense of discomfort with difference and with the unexpected. Getting it right makes all the difference in the world.

TWO

Jesus Heals Everyone He Meets

I recently asked a group of pastors what they thought the Bible had to say about disability. One Catholic priest raised his hand and said, "Well, Jesus heals everyone he meets!" Being in a Roman Catholic context, there was a crucifix on the wall with a very bloody, wounded, and nearly dead Jesus depicted on it. Indicating the crucifix, I asked the priest, "Just so I'm clear: How are you defining the term 'disability'? Would you say that a body in the state of Jesus there should be called disabled?"

"No," he said, "Jesus is only injured." For this priest, Jesus was only three days away from being restored to normality—just as he had restored so many people to normality in the course of his ministry. Such pastors make disabled people very nervous. A Jesus determined to miraculously make everyone "normal" feels threatening to most disabled people.

Fortunately, this is not the Jesus we find in the Bible.

Good News in the Bible for Disabled Readers

In a 2019 radio episode called "Pick Up Your Stretcher and Walk," the blind journalist Damon Rose interviewed Becky Tyler, a Christian sixteen-year-old with quadriplegic cerebral palsy.[1] In the show

29

Rose puzzles through why Christians sometimes approach him on the street in London and offer to pray over him for healing. Rose has come to terms with his blindness as part of who he is, is comfortable with it, and is living a very full life as a journalist for the BBC.

Rose is not a believer. In the radio show he wonders why Christians seem unable to imagine that he might be comfortable with his blindness. Rose feels bemusement and a little frustration about the Christian inability to accept the idea that he might be perfectly happy and well-adjusted as a blind person. This is a puzzle he cannot let go—why does this seem to be so deeply embedded in the Christian view of the world?

He has read the Gospels, and it's true: Jesus does seem to eradicate every disability that he meets. So does following Jesus commit Christians to believing that all disabilities will sooner or later be eradicated?

Rose puts this question to Becky, the Christian teenager with cerebral palsy. Becky has never been able to walk. She is now in a wheelchair that cradles her body in a lying position, held in by straps. Here's what she had to say in answer to Rose's question.

> When I was about twelve years old, I was feeling sad because I felt God didn't love me as much as other people, because I am in a wheelchair and I can't do lots of things other people can do. I felt this way because I did not see anyone with a wheelchair in the Bible, and nearly all the disabled people in the Bible get healed by Jesus. So, they are not like me. I asked God about it, but I didn't hear God talk to me about it straight away. I told my mum how I was feeling, and my mum showed me a verse from the Bible in the book of Daniel, chapter seven verse nine, which basically says God's throne has wheels. So, God has a wheelchair! In fact, it's not just any old chair, it's the best chair in the Bible! It's God's throne and it's a wheelchair! This made me feel like God understands what it's like to have a wheelchair, and that having a wheelchair is actually very cool, because God has one and not so many people can say that! I have a silly picture in my head of God flying around heaven in a gold sparkly throne, a bit like a caped superhero might fly through the sky, powered by his thoughts and variously strategically placed jet packs. I'm sure that's not at all scriptural, but it sounds like fun!

Biblical scholar Candida Moss suggests that Becky might be more right than she suspects.[2] In Genesis, God walks in the garden with Adam and Eve. Yet the writer of Ezekiel 1 is equally comfortable depicting God moving about on a wheeled throne. In Ezekiel, God sits down and does not need or want to get up again. In his vision, Ezekiel does see God moving about on a fantastical throne powered by God's thoughts and carried on wings, if not propelled by jets as Becky has imagined.

While the eternal God perhaps does not have a body of this type, it is nevertheless remarkable that one thousand years before the invention of the wheelchair, ancient Israelites are imagining a chair with wheels as a suitable way for God to appear in public. Taken in its ancient context, Moss points out, the sheer cultural incongruity of the image allows us to say that for Ezekiel, as for Daniel, God is a wheelchair user.

For Becky, at least, this is a healing reading. God has pronounced her beloved as she is—no matter what other Christians might think.

A Blind Man Walks into a Church . . .

"A blind man walks into a church . . ." We recognize this as the opening of a joke. Jokes draw mirth from awkwardness not easily spoken about. The awkwardness that is the subject of this book is one that the church nevertheless *needs* to speak about. When a blind person walks into a church, we can be pretty sure they feel the discomfort this joke is begging us to notice.

To address the reasons for this discomfort demands revisiting taken-for-granted readings of Scripture. If we can work out why a blind person feels uncomfortable coming into church, we will have taken several decisive steps toward discerning how to think *Christianly* about disability.

The comment from the priest with which this chapter opened represents one of the most common ways among Christians of understanding the relation of the Bible, Jesus, and disability. An obvious reason why people come up and pray over disabled people for healing is that this is what Jesus seems to be continually doing in the Gospels.

As we will soon see in more detail, a closer reading of how blindness functions in the New Testament reveals that most references to it are not *really* about blindness but are using a *physical* condition to highlight a problematic *spiritual* condition, an alienation from reality. When the Gospel writers speak about blindness, they very often employ an old and widespread ancient trope used throughout the ancient world. Today that ancient way of speaking of a spiritual condition by using a disability as a stand-in for a spiritual deficit has become more problematic.

Christians today need to revisit the assumption that to be blind is to be broken, deficient, or not normal. We need to do so if we want to squarely face the discomfort disabled people feel in church today. We need to understand how we can affirm the concern of the scriptural writers to use conditions like blindness to highlight the problem of being *unrepentant* while at the same time attending to the social ostracization that attended the physical state of blindness and other bodily conditions in the ancient world.

There are good pastoral reasons to engage in this critical examination of how we have understood the Bible. It is important to find ways to resist the impulse to categorize the disabled people in our midst within the narrow options we remember from the Bible. We must learn to ask instead: "Which story with God is *this* person living?" The Bible offers Christians a whole catalog of stories whose contours help believers in every age recognize what God might be doing in someone's life. As we will soon see, sometimes God even disables people or refuses their requests to be cured, alongside sometimes performing miraculous healings.

Biblical stories fundamentally orient Christian discernment. Thus when we Christians think that only a handful of healing stories are what the Bible says about disability, our capacity to discern what God is doing in different lives is distorted. Christian discernment requires at least that we deepen our awareness of the range of disability stories in Scripture. It also demands that we attend to people where they are, to *discover* what God is doing in and through them.

To see a disabled person coming into church through a narrow handful of Gospel healing stories short-circuits the all-important work of Christian discernment.

We don't immediately assume of a wealthy person entering church that they need to repent, as is true of most of the stories told about rich people in the Gospels. Nor, when we find out that someone is a theologian, do we immediately assume that all the bad things that Jesus said about the scribes apply to them (though they certainly may!).

This chapter is designed to help Christians out of habitually connecting people in church with the healing stories in the Gospels— which, as we will see, are themselves far richer than we often assume.

What the Bible helps us see about disability will not be learned by tracking the biblical stories *about* that small number of disabled people who get healed. Only once we have asked wider questions about what the Bible really says about disabling conditions will we be prepared to return to these well-known healing stories ready to attend to them again in their full biblical context.

We also need to attend to what it means that we are *all* living as inhabitants of the modern developed world. The modern intellectual context offers Christians a limited number of scripts through which to see disability, its problems, and its solutions. The first way the Bible helps us to think better about disability is in revealing how limited those scripts are.

Disrupting the stories we have inherited from the people around us is how the Holy Spirit has always incorporated people into the people of God. Sanctification means discovering our place in the ongoing story God is writing with the world, learning to see our continuities with that one great and multifaceted story told in the many stories of Scripture.

Disability has certainly been interpreted in a range of problematic ways in the churches over the centuries. Yet it has also pressed Christians to read Scripture in exciting and fresh ways. Christians must be prepared to hear the discomfort of people with disabilities as they read much of the Bible. What the Bible explicitly says about disability *is* full of ambiguities and difficulties.

Taking the Bible seriously on the topic of disability today, affirming it yet again as members of the body of Christ, means embracing it in all its angularity as the central source of Christian theology. Staying with it, and also with those among us whom it makes feel uncomfortable, forces contemporary Christians to return once again to their sacred texts from a new and unexpected angle. Christians undertake this work out of the desire to stay true to the healing and life-giving works of Jesus. This is the promise of letting the human experience of disability reveal how much is actually in the Bible.

Christians' Many Views of Disability

Let me explain how this works by relating a conversation with my friend Chantal Huinink. Slightly older than Becky (though I won't say how much!), Chantal is a Christian woman with cerebral palsy. Chantal's mind is razor sharp, but her body doesn't always follow directions. This leads to speech and vision problems as well as difficulties controlling her arms and legs. She has never walked and now, like Becky, gets around in a motorized wheelchair.

When Chantal was young, her mother introduced her to an album of music by Joni Eareckson Tada, another Christian in a wheelchair. Joni became quadriplegic after breaking her neck in a diving accident as a teenager. In the course of coming to terms with her disability experience and making peace with her new life as a quadriplegic, Joni came to a vibrant faith.

Not too many years after her accident, Joni become a major author and evangelist, as well as the founder of Joni and Friends, a ministry with a worldwide reach that serves people with disabilities. She also wanted to share her story and the gospel that had become so life giving to her. In 1985 she sang the vocals on an album of children's songs aimed at helping young children come to terms with their own disabilities—and their faith.[3]

Joni's life and testimony were chronicled in the feature-length film *Joni*,[4] which was screened in hundreds of churches across the US in the 1980s. The film traces Joni's youth, her accident, her recovery process in traction in the hospital, and her journey with God through it all.

I told Chantal that seeing this movie in church as a junior high kid was my first direct engagement with the intersection of disability and faith. The movie had genuinely unsettled me. I was horrified by the scene in which Joni was fitted with a halo that drove pins into her skull in order to hold her neck still during traction. Her protracted suspension in the contraption that immobilized her spine as it healed seemed the closest thing to a modern torturer's rack I had ever encountered.

The specter of becoming paralyzed—and the harrowing vision of the hospital tortures that would follow—had simply overwhelmed my twelve-year-old capacity to hear the good news of the faith that was sprouting in all this pain and loss. My projection of my own horror at becoming paralyzed and living in a wheelchair was simply too powerful.

The film beautifully depicts Joni's lively spirit and creativity. It ends showing her doing amazing watercolors with a brush held in her mouth. It was all too easy, however, for a powerful emotional experience of the film to link up with the intentionally harrowing A Thief in the Night movie series that also made the rounds of churches in the 1980s—terrifying the youth of my church.[5] Even if the tribulations of the hospital and the four horsemen of the apocalypse all end in Christian bliss, they are nevertheless life courses that both films powerfully suggest the viewer should do everything in their power to avoid.

When I told Chantal how the Joni movie had painted my first emotional responses to the theme of God and disability, she was genuinely shocked at what I'd felt. How could anyone experience Joni's story as anything but heart-warming and empowering? I explained to her how, for me, the emotional impact of projected *loss* had simply drowned out the message of newborn faith that was woven through the film. I was as likely to have heard the gospel story that was plainly there in all the horror as to have a phone conversation at a rock concert.

Chantal replied that since she had been in the hospital many times and had *never* walked, the loss of the capacity to walk and the trauma of hospital treatment had not stuck out in her memory at all. The songs she had learned from Joni as a child, in contrast, had offered her a deeply life-giving gospel, showing her how to have a confident and trusting faith even in a wheelchair. In the years to come Chantal had not only gotten to know Joni but had become her friend.

Yet these heaven-bound wheelchair-using Christians had slightly different hopes for the resurrection. Joni, whose quadriplegia was acquired, looks forward to being able to walk again in her resurrection body. "More than the ability to walk, I think I would like a wheel-chair equipped with jet packs!" Chantal said with a laugh. The truth is, the form of her resurrection body is not the center of Chantal's faith.

The most important moment in Chantal's Christian life happened in the run-up to a youth group field trip. The youth group was headed out for a fun weekend excursion. Though Chantal really wanted to go, she sacrificially offered to stay behind, having learned that the church had been unable to find a wheelchair-accessible bus. When the teens in the youth group found out Chantal was not going to come, they responded in one voice: "No way! We're not going without Chantal! We want you with us, and we will lift you and your chair up onto the bus ourselves."

Chantal discovered that she was loved and wanted just as she was. She found herself in the love of the body of Christ that was prepared to wait for one another. This was the healing miracle of Jesus in her life. It was a healing embrace, and it happened without Chantal being made "normal."

The Many Narratives of Disability Experience

Let's plot the stories I've told in this chapter within the biblical universe.

Consider Joni's and Chantal's different perspectives about whether it is desirable to walk in heaven. Joni's desire to walk again suggests that her story with God has traveled a Mephibosheth trajectory. Joni's walk with God has been a journey of coming to terms with a body whose functioning has been permanently diminished because of mistakes or foolish decisions made by people in the past. Coming to terms with where God is in regret, loss, and suffering were thus necessary parts of her journey of faith.

Chantal, in contrast, has always welcomed her existence, including her body, as a gift from God. Chantal's spiritual journey was from feeling like an outsider in not being a "normal" teenager to discovering that in Christ's body, the church, she is genuinely an indispensable part. The welcome of the body of Christ challenged her internalized desire to protect her feelings by refusing to reveal her need for physical help and for social belonging.

My story differs from both Joni's and Chantal's. In my fear of losing my physical capacity and of hospitals, I was confronting the possibility that the road God had for me to travel might *cost* me something. Like Jacob wrestling with the man at the ford of the Jabbok, not knowing if he would be killed, this loss challenged my view of the salvation I could hope for from Jesus. That biblical story confronts the believer with the question of how we will respond to *good* news when it arrives looking very much like *bad* news.

The conversation I had with Chantal about the movie followed yet another narrative logic: that of learning something unexpected *from* someone unexpected. I could not believe how different our experiences of the movie had been, and I felt genuinely enlightened by hearing Chantal's reading, which gave me a whole new view of my own reactions, God, and disability. She said the same about hearing mine.

Neither Chantal nor I had previously ever been able to imagine the other's experiences. But as brother and sister in the body of Christ, we had been drawn into a relationship in which genuinely different life experiences could be not only heard but learned from. By being close enough to talk, in knowing we were bound in one body, we were able to trust and open up, and we both were changed.

Jesus was a master of creating this reversal of expectations with his stories and parables about a kingdom that is spoken most truly from the mouths of little children. The theme of reversals of expectation provides an important clue about how to read Jesus's parables about blindness. Jesus's central concern in his interactions with blind people is to teach sighted people the truths that they are too distracted to see but that the blind people around Jesus *see all too clearly.*

I have connected these different aspects of the stories told in this section to different biblical stories in order to highlight that *there is no easy or single way to connect Scripture with any given disability.* Nor is there a single trajectory through the disability experience.

Every person is living through a moment in God's story whose dynamics can be appreciated by one or another facet of the biblical text. But the relevant biblical story can only be one that meets the many unique features and contours of each person's life. These unique contours also change over time. The biblical passages through which God will free and move any given believer forward at any given point in their life will not necessarily be the ones that we, or anyone else, were expecting.

To be a Christian is to be learning to live the truths and stories of Scripture in our own places and in our own bodies. God has one story, but that story unfurls in magnificently particular ways in the intimate spaces of our own times and places.

The Threat and Embarrassment of the Bible

Christians having an impoverished catalog of biblical stories to guide their discernment produces a misshapen perception of the lives of people undergoing the disability experience. John Swinton explains why this is a problem.

> I always remember the experience of a friend of mine, Monica, who has severe cerebral palsy that affects her speech and her mobility. She is someone who loves Jesus deeply. A few years ago she went to a healing service in my home town of Aberdeen in Scotland. At one point she went forward for healing. She had been experiencing really debilitating back pains for a number of weeks and wanted to ask God to alleviate her condition. She went forward. However, before she had time to explain her back issue, the pastor began to pray for the release of the demons that had caused her to become "a cripple" and that had "taken her speech from her." Needless to say she left: angry, upset, alienated, and humiliated.[6]

We can glimpse through stories like these many missed opportunities—to read the Bible differently, to engage with suffering congregants differently, and to think again what the Gospels mean when they depict Jesus healing people. Swinton observes, "Perhaps if the pastor had taken time to get to know Monica and to understand that she lived a peaceful shalomic life with Jesus, within which her apparent impairments were not a problem for her, he might have been able to use whatever gifts of healing he may have had in a way that was faithful and peaceful. In so doing he would have been able to reveal something truthful about Jesus."[7]

I have no doubt that Christians—especially pastors—want to "reveal something true about Jesus," as Swinton so aptly puts it. But revealing Jesus truly entails facing the reality that the pastoral misuse of the Bible has made many disabled people experience the Bible as threatening or embarrassing.

Sometimes the threat of Scripture comes by way of pastoral performances of Scripture that are tone deaf and humiliating, as it did for Monica. Other times, however, the Scriptures strike directly. We have listened to Frances Young before, the theologian and mother of Arthur, who has cerebral palsy and substantial learning impairment. For years she struggled not only with the sheer workload of being both a professional and a carer for Arthur but also with why God allowed Arthur to suffer the deprivation of oxygen in the womb that led to his disabilities.

One Sunday as she was wrestling with the question of why evil comes into the world, Young heard John 9:3 read out from the pulpit: "It was not that this man sinned, or his parents, but that the works of God might be manifest in him." Young writes, "'What an appalling statement!' I thought. Could it really be suggested that that man and his family had to put up with all those years of disability just so Jesus could wave a magic wand and heal him to demonstrate his power? I found myself protesting with all the protest generated by Arthur."[8]

John Hull had to face these questions in the most pointed way when, as an academic theologian, he began to lose his vision in his late thirties. In his book *In the Beginning There Was Darkness*, he recounts how he had to learn everything again: how to read, how to negotiate once-familiar spaces, how to get around when no longer able to drive or cycle. In the course of this laborious retraining, Hull found himself increasingly frustrated by the way blind people are described in the Bible, as they often seem to be treated as inferior, as lacking.

The story of Sodom and Gomorrah (Gen. 19:4–11), for instance, sets up a link between blindness and sexual violence. This theme of blindness being visited on sinners as a punishment is vividly present in the New Testament, as when a Jewish false prophet is blinded as punishment by the disciples (Acts 13:6–13). Such narrative portrayals of blindness being meted out as a punishment for sin are defended more directly in passages such as Job 5:12–14; 17:5; 22:11; Psalms 38:10; 69:23; Isaiah 59:9–10, 12; Zephaniah 1:17; and Zechariah 11:17. If this is not bad enough, there are biblical exemplars of calling someone blind as a term of ridicule and abuse, as in Isaiah 56:10 and 2 Samuel 5:6–8.

Hull asks readers to consider what this dominant understanding of blindness must have meant for those in its original context—and how it can be threatening to disabled readers today.

> The psychological effects of all this on those who were without sight must have been horrific. The estimate which blind people form of themselves is a mirror image of the view of blindness held in the surrounding society. If you have always consciously or unconsciously thought of blind people as pathetic and incompetent, when you become blind yourself you adopt an image of yourself as pathetic and incompetent. One of the most common reasons for disabled people losing their jobs is the low self-image which is the result of the initial impact of their disability, a low image with which their employer readily concurs.[9]

Sometimes Christians' inability to speak intelligently about biblical portrayals of disability just ends up being downright embarrassing, as it was for Joan, who is from Nashville, Tennessee.

> Years ago I had a back surgery for scoliosis that called for a body cast for six months. . . . Years passed, and now I bend forward badly and can only walk with a walker to stabilize myself. The bending forward and knees buckling are a result of complications from the surgery years before. . . . Recently we were attending a church that was over an hour away from our home but had a visiting preacher that my husband and I enjoyed hearing who would be there on three consecutive Sundays. We were warmly greeted all three Sundays by the small but welcoming congregation. The sermons were to be from the Gospel of John. The retired preacher from a large church had once spent three years covering the entire book of John on Sundays, and he was tremendously gifted in breadth of knowledge and information recall. On the third of his three Sundays preaching, the text he chose was about the woman with the bent back. As he spoke, the situation became more and more embarrassing as he described and talked of

this woman, with great detail about hems of dresses and other necessary care the woman would have needed.

With his vast base of sermons that he knew well, and knowing I would be in the audience, why this one? The sermon had made many feel very uncomfortable. That Sunday he left quicker than usual and even the congregation did not usually depart as fast as they did this Sunday! No one spoke to us after this sermon. Embarrassment seemed to reign for us all.[10]

One can only assume the best, that the preacher in question thought he would be recognizing the woman's condition by preaching a sermon that seemed to contain a character in a similar condition. But with all his study and erudition, he made the simple error of assuming that people's disabilities are the best way to link them with Scripture. And he did it before a congregation that had no idea how to respond to his obvious mistake.

The result is a familiar one to people with disabilities who go to church—no one dared to speak to the person with the disability who had been so unfairly singled out. The congregation, beset by the hesitation blues, scurried away. Embarrassment reigned. How can we do better?

Learning from Disabled Readers

The first and most important way out of the reign of embarrassment, misunderstanding, and offense that characterizes the relationship of the church to disabled people is to start listening to them. "Christian churches need the wisdom and struggle of disabled lives," notes Rebecca Spurrier, "to help them interpret anew their holy texts and body practices, their traditions of gathering, their symbols and sacraments, in order to grasp the latent truths suppressed through segregation and stigma."[11] As the stories in this chapter have amply illustrated, different life experiences make for different sensitivities to aspects of the biblical texts that are often overlooked.

Grant Macaskill has recently highlighted what autistic readers have seen in Scripture that others have not seen before. Using his perspective as a professor of New Testament, Macaskill makes clear the senses in which the "autistic eye" might well see more of what is actually in the text, may hew more closely to the way the words run. It is likely, if not verifiable, that some of the great exegetes of the past may have been autistic, and there are certainly biblical scholars today—not to mention pastors—whose success springs from their autism, observes Macaskill.

> There may be other, less stark examples of autistic interpretation or theology that benefit the church on a weekly basis through the preaching of pastors with autism. I am aware of at least one such pastor, who is open about his autism and ministers to his congregation in a way that embraces it. I am sure there are countless others of whom I am unaware, and that these numbers will continue to grow as rates of diagnosis begin to catch up with the reality of the life of the church. The serious study of their sermons or teachings could add to our knowledge of how autistic individuals read the Bible in ways that are beneficial for the community as a whole.[12]

Too often Christians have positioned themselves to relate to disabled people as the ones who know the truth and who know what disabled people need. The stories related in this chapter make it painfully clear how likely that stance is to lead to offense to those among us who already face stares and questions on a daily basis. Even more importantly, a church that does not recognize its disabled members as intrinsic to itself is cutting off parts of the body of Christ. And as it does so, it cuts itself off from the full richness of the Bible's description of new life in that body, which is enriched precisely in learning to overcome the estrangement of difference.

Fox summarizes why the faithfulness of contemporary Christians' reading of the Bible depends on listening to disabled voices.

> When interpreters honor and include the perspectives and experiences of people with disabilities, their careful attention to the characterizations and personalities of those Jesus heals draws out aspects of the healing narratives that are sometimes overlooked. Often these interpreters notice that what disables the people seeking healing has at least as much to do with social and cultural factors as it does with their physical limitations. . . . Many obstacles facing people with disabilities

are socially constructed both in Jesus' context and today, so a lens that acknowledges how this impacts life before and after a healing is essential for interpreting the healing narratives and developing holistic practices of healing in our church communities.[13]

We are going to spend more time with the Ethiopian eunuch whom the Spirit leads Philip to evangelize. For now, recall that this man, riding in his wheeled chariot—like God in Ezekiel and Becky, Chantal, and Joni in this chapter—invited Philip to join him on the chariot.

Let's pause to think of ourselves as a bit like the Ethiopian eunuch. His question is a gateway to taking the disability experience seriously: "How can I [understand], unless someone guides me?" (Acts 8:31 NRSV). There is nothing more powerful than letting ourselves sit down beside those who are publicly known for being visibly different. What might it mean to sit alongside him and ask what we might learn about the Bible and Christian faith from him and the fellow believers whose life experiences are so different from our own?

The remainder of this chapter is intended not as an exhaustive treatment of what the Bible has to say about disability but of what readers with an experience of disability might reveal about what the Bible actually says.

On Curing and Healing

All roads seem to lead to the question of how we imagine Jesus to have done his healing, so it would be best to begin here.

The problem is that our cultural distance from life thousands of years ago makes it especially hard to read the healing narratives rightly. We read the Gospels through our own experiences of medicine, hospitals, and healing. Our commonsense knowledge of how medical care works today affects which details of the biblical story we notice and which we do not. It also shapes which aspects of Jesus's healing narratives we assume to be part of his work of healing.

"In the West, most of us operate with a biomedical lens unless we intentionally privilege another viewpoint," observes Fox.[14] She substantiates this claim by surveying the readings of Jesus's healing by five doctors, comparing their readings with those of eight people who share the disability experience. What immediately becomes clear is that those readers who have disability experiences notice many more details of what is actually in the biblical narratives. This is very powerful: being "normal" may in fact render Christians lazy and inattentive readers of Scripture. This is why climbing up in the chariot with the Ethiopian eunuch—and with Becky and Chantal—promises not only to help us understand disability but to help us understand *what it means to be church*.

Disabled readers make a very obvious point. Jesus does not in fact heal everyone he meets. Nor does he heal as a matter of course even those who come to him. His healings are never felt to be intrusive, unwanted, or embarrassing. And they not only restore people's bodies but restore their relationships with other people.

Modern readers, schooled to think of bodies and healings like doctors do today, don't see how different ancient views of healing are from our medical assumptions. Decades ago George Engel had already clarified the problems with what has become the "folk model" of modern Western society. Fox explains, "On the whole, Westerners tend to think of illness as something biological that happens to individuals, and the practice of medicine as geared toward curing the disease by finding the bodily cause and addressing it directly. In ancient Mediterranean culture, however, illness is not thought of in purely bodily terms, nor is it something that effects only an individual."[15]

Because the medical model "assumes disease to be fully accounted for by deviations from the norm of measurable biological (somatic) variables"[16] and that all such conditions are undesirable, the role of medicine is always to offer corrective treatments to alleviate discomfort and impairments. To read the healing narratives well today we must therefore try to set aside some very deep-seated assumptions that tend to make us misread them.

First, when we think of medicine, we think within a paradigm in which medicine is a scientific pursuit that aims at curing sicknesses. The dominance of this way of conceiving of medicine is indicated by the fact that all other forms of healing practice are considered "alternative medicine"—that is, alternative to the "real" medicine learned in medical schools today.

Second, the premise of biomedicine is that the individual person's body is the locus of sickness and the focal point of healing. This means that modern medicine individualizes bodies and illnesses. This second premise is the source of what is increasingly called "medicalization," the tendency to see any human illness as something that has gone wrong with the body, no matter how it came about. Even if we become sick because of living in poverty or being abused at home or at work, biomedicine focuses solely on the individual body and tries to get it working "normally."

Third, biomedicine emphasizes the patient's responsibility for necessary lifestyle changes. Other cultures (such as the one Jesus lived in) often have more collectivist understandings of how health and sickness operate, and who makes decisions about treatment.

Fourth, the modern medical professional tends to strike a stance of scientific objectivity. Conversations are brief and professional, treatment is expected to be the best available, and emotional connections are avoided between doctor and patient. Here modern medicine could not be further from Jesus, who is clearly emotionally engaged with those around him and those whose "treatments" are often incidentally offered as more life-changing personal bonds are forming.

Fifth, modern doctors have increasingly narrow domains of expertise. They treat parts and individual systems. They do not, and cannot, address the whole person, in all of their body, let alone all of their life.

In sum, modern medicine locates sickness in a single physical body or even in single parts of bodies. It then aims to cure these bodies without reference to the social and psychic context in which they exist, keeping professional distance from the persons being cured while curing them. This could hardly be a more different view of healing than what we see in the Gospels.

It is certainly true that the early Christians invented the hospital as we know it[17] and that there are Christians today who care more holistically for people than the biomedical framework presumes. But the evidence is overwhelming that when most Christians read the Gospels today, they often default to the view that Jesus heals everyone he meets.

Jesus as Restorer

One difference between modern medical curing and Jesus's healing activity is so obvious it is hard to believe it has been so long over-looked. Not once does Jesus heal someone who does not cry out to him.

Jesus shows an amazing sensitivity to the context of the people who approach him. People today approach a doctor for one thing, but people approach Jesus for all kinds of reasons and with all kinds of aims in mind, and he knows this.

Jesus sometimes commands people who sought nothing from him to follow him (Mark 2:14). Yes, it is true, once in a while he unilaterally liberates people from demons (1:25) or cleanses the sin of those who are willing (2:5). From Jesus's perspective, every human being is in need of having their sins forgiven, having their bodies healed, and being liberated from malevolent agency-robbing powers. Jesus's words and presence bring the universal hope of every human being to specific people and their specific needs.

Yet this healing work is multilayered. The different Gospel writers bring out different aspects of the redemptive work of Jesus.

Mark, for instance, highlights Jesus's intense attentiveness to the desires of those who come to him. Jesus heals in recognition of the desire of people who have brought the sick and possessed and physically lame to Jesus for their liberation and healing (1:30–34; 2:3).

Nowhere is this focus on Jesus's responsivity to human need reduced to his seeking out "illnesses needing to be cured." Instead Jesus responds to the crying desire of those who come to him. Mark highlights this feature of Jesus's redemptive work in his very first chapter by telling the story of a man with leprosy who "came to Jesus and begged him on his knees" (1:40). Notice that the man begs not to be cured but to be made clean. This is a ritual designation. To be made clean means to be able to rejoin the community of the faithful, to be readmitted into Israel's worship by the priests.

Jesus does not respond by simply healing him, as a doctor would have. Instead he replies that he is willing to make him clean. His healing act is to say, "Be clean!" (Mark 1:41). The next verse says, "Immediately the leprosy left him and he was cleansed" (1:42).

Mark very cleverly focuses his hearer's attention on the religious problem associated with a specific illness, *without* equating that biological illness with the real request of the man. The man does *not* ask to be "cured," and Jesus hears what he *actually* asks. He grants what he actually asks: readmission to the religious community. But to do so he has to cure his leprosy.

We don't really know what this meant, of course. We can't know if the ravaged digits and appendages that are characteristic of untreated leprosy were miraculously healed or reconstituted. These types of modern-medical questions are not the point of the story. The disease has been stopped and in a way that will satisfy the religious authorities.

The disease has been wiped away not because the man asked for a cure but because the man, using specifically coded religious language, asked someone he believed was at least a powerful rabbi to allow him to come back into full fellowship with the community of faith. "Moved with compassion, Jesus stretched out His hand and touched him, and said to him, 'I am willing; be cleansed'" (1:41 NASB). Jesus is attuned to the yearning of a child of Israel cut off from life in the worshiping community. To restore this man will mean healing him, and this is something Jesus is willing to do.

The implications of the story are clear. Unlike modern medicine, which regularly says it wants to "eradicate" this or that disease, Jesus is not wandering the ancient Near East seeking to restore everybody that he meets to normal biological functioning.

Jesus redeems people who cry out to him for help. And sometimes he heals them. As a member of a cultural context in which certain illnesses and disabilities rendered their bearers social and religious outcasts, Jesus was bound to meet people suffering because of their condition, and he responded to this suffering.

I can't end this section on the problem of the social exclusion of people with disability in the ancient world without drawing attention to an Old Testament parable of the kingdom, from 2 Kings 7. The hostile Aramean army has been besieging Samaria, the capital city of Israel. The siege has been going on so long that people are starving.

Being a leper meant being ritually unclean, and it also meant being barred from entering the city gates. Even during a siege, the lepers remain outside the gates, and they too are starving. Not only are they rejected by the city, but they are threatened by an enemy army. Finally, four of them have had enough. Their living death has got to end. "They said to each other, 'Why stay here until we die? If we say, 'We'll go into the city'—the famine is there, and we will die. And if we stay here, we will die. So let's go over to the camp of the Arameans and surrender. If they spare us, we live; if they kill us, then we die'" (2 Kings 7:3b–4).

But earlier in the night God so frightened the Aramean army that they had fled without any of their tents or supplies. The four lepers are the first witnesses of the bounty of the Lord's deliverance. First they feast. Then they take a few things. Then they feast again. Before the sun rises, however, they realize: "What we're doing is not right. This is a day of good news and we are keeping it to ourselves" (2 Kings 7:9). They go back to the city and announce to the gate-keepers that the Aramaeans have abandoned their tents and, more importantly, all their food. Thus do four lepers, the excluded in Israel, become the first to dine at the table that has been left by God's redeeming hand. Thus do these, the excluded in Israel, become the ones chosen to announce God's salvation.

In these four lepers we are also presented with a prefiguration of the message that Paul will hold out as the essence of the church's relation to disability. These four lepers point forward to the church in seeing that faithfully receiving God's bounty means learning to wait for one another. Even those responsible for their exclusion deserve to have a place at the table God has set for Israel.

The last have become first—in living out what it means to be part of God's people.

Mercy, Not Healing

Jesus's miracles bring people together. What he does not do is assume that everyone he meets wants nothing more than to be "normal." Nor does he set up a stall, like traveling faith healers, to invite people to be healed in front of a crowd. Jesus is the one being approached on the street, as it were.

Another story from Mark makes this clear. The story is of Jesus healing the man who has come to be called "blind" Bartimaeus (10:46–52). Bartimaeus, like the man in Mark's first chapter, does not say,

"Jesus, come here and heal me." Instead, his language is clearly religious: "Jesus, Son of David, have mercy on me!" (10:47).

Mercy, not healing.

Could I interject here by making an obvious point about the blatant misreading of this passage? If you think that this is a story about a man coming to Jesus to be cured of blindness, try his line with your doctor. The doctor might hear you, but you will probably be offered psychiatric help.

Jesus hears the request as a confession of faith in him as the messiah. It represents a confession of Jesus as God because no Jewish—or Greek or Roman—healer had ever been rumored to have healed blindness. Bartimaeus is asking for the impossible. Because Jesus hears all this in Bartimaeus's cry, he does not assume that one who has done what every human should do, who sees what every human desperately needs to see, needs anything more. For someone who has seen the messiah, what more can having sight add?

So Jesus asks: "What do you want me to do for you?" (Mark 10:51). He never asks this question of the disciples he calls or of those possessed by powers that rob them of their agency.

The crowd watching was no doubt watching with bated breath as they screamed in their heads, "He wants to see, obviously!" Jesus himself does not assume this. And that he does not is the key to understanding what makes Jesus so different from the modern doctor.

Jesus does not assume. Jesus does not assume that one who sees him as the messiah wants what society says they should want. On the contrary.

Though he does not assume that the man wants his eyes to be changed, he knows that in this place and time to be blind was to be excluded from society. So Jesus extends the mercy on this man who has asked for nothing more. Jesus has mercy on him in the terms of the society in which Bartimaeus would have to live out his faith. He restores him to live in society by giving him that kind of sight that most people have and which society so values.

But Jesus knows: he knows that Bartimaeus has seen something as a blind person that is more important than what the sighted can see. And it is Bartimaeus's seeing and confessing this to which Jesus responds by restoring Bartimaeus to life as a full member of society.[18]

Would Jesus need to restore the sight of the blind in our society today? What we know from this story, Hull comments, is that "Jesus offers the man the dignity and independence of declaring his request. Nowadays, the blind person would have said, 'Get me some computer training and a job with a firm that has a decent equal opportunities policy', but this story is not set in the modern world. Bartimaeus says, 'Master, let me receive my sight.'"[19] It is a sign of our colonization by the medical model of healing that most Christians' first response to Hull's reading of the story would be to deny it: "Of course Jesus wanted to heal his eyes!"

As Fox points out, however, such a response assumes that what the man came to Jesus for was to have his eyes cured, restored to normalcy.[20] It also makes the pastorally disastrous assumption that Jesus did not need to ask what Bartimaeus actually wanted. That is not what the text says. It is a projection of what we as Western, medicalized readers would want from Jesus.

Hull teaches us to read more closely. And in doing so he provokes the church to reconsider whether its reading of the story is sufficiently attentive to the full richness of Scripture.

The Nonverbal Jesus

Let's stay with the theme of blindness. Focusing on blindness offers us a better handle on the problem of the offensive nature of the cultural stereotypes that Jesus seems to be upholding. Jesus could have changed all society to make it more welcoming of people with sensory impairments. Instead he restored Bartimaeus's sight rather than directly confronting the injustice of a society that ostracized people with certain physical conditions and illnesses.

Recall that what is central to all of the Gospels is the emphasis on the blessedness of those who believe in Jesus's name, especially without seeing him (John 20:29).

In his own teaching Jesus sometimes draws on stories and teachings that assume the superiority of a sighted perspective (such as Matt. 5:14–16) while other times he tells stories and teaches in ways that are more tactile and aurally oriented (5:30). Sometimes in his stories hands can become eyes and vice versa.

In short, the Gospel writers present Jesus as a tactile and compassionate person who nevertheless uses the term "blind" as an insult in ways that remain painful to blind readers today (as in Matt. 23:16–17, 19, 24, 26).

Perhaps more importantly, Jesus himself submitted to being divinely robbed of sight, as Adam Booth observes: "While it is a much shorter experience of sightlessness, Jesus is blind-folded during his Passion (Luke 22:63–65). [Louise] Lawrence, while noting that this is 'not the same as blindness,' notes that it is 'nevertheless an experience that renders him temporarily sightless and brings some solidarity with this state.' . . . Right before his death, Jesus becomes (at least partially) sightless for a completely different reason: the sun's light fails and the whole land is covered in darkness (Luke 23:44–45)."[21]

Jesus involuntarily suffering sightlessness is the key to circumventing the offense some of his assumptions about blind people can cause to blind people today. Hull writes,

> "Blessed are those who are not offended." Jesus used imagery offensive to blind people, but at the same time did not resist himself being immersed in blindness on the cross out of love for us (Lk 22:64). It is because, however briefly, he shares in our condition, undergoing mockery and a humiliation that few of us have had to undergo, that we cannot be offended at him. Dear Master . . . I do not ask you to heal me but only that if you call me to follow you in blindness, you will hold my hand.[22]

Let us linger for a moment with this prayer, for the prayer of the Christian is not something to be taken lightly. Hull is blind. As he cries out to God, he intentionally echoes the formulation of Bartimaeus. He addresses Jesus as his "dear Master." Like Bartimaeus before the crowd, Hull expresses before his readers the desire of his heart. And he does so toward the same Jesus who so long ago responded to Bartimaeus with compassion.

"Dear Master . . . I do not ask you to heal me but only that if you call me to follow you in blindness, you will hold my hand."

We need to stop for a moment and sit with this prayer. Christians need to feel the emotional weight of what they do if they instinctively respond to this prayer, "You do not have enough faith. Jesus can and wants to heal you, as he healed those around him." Hull asks not for healing but for Jesus's presence in the blindness he has accepted as God's way for him. That this makes some of us uncomfortable reveals something critical about our own assumptions about what he *should* be asking for. We tacitly assume that we can deny Hull's right to place himself alongside Bartimaeus and make his own request to his master.

When we do this, we express not the hope for healing and mercy that is depicted in the Gospels but the assumptions of an age that has been trained to see some bodies as good and normally functioning and others as broken and in need of a fix. We overlay on the Gospels a medical picture of healing that assumes we know what it looks like for bodies to be well functioning and that has no wider goals than to restore that functioning.

When we deny Hull this prayer, we thus express our complicity in the ways of the world that make it difficult for people with disabilities to come to church. Despite being Christians, we channel the world of medical science, which perceives people according to hierarchies of skills and capacities.

The Bible has something for those of us who find ourselves in this position too. It is a prayer.

> Be gracious to us, be gracious,
> Because we've become very full of contempt.
> Our entire being has become very full for itself
> Of the ridicule of complacent people,
> Of the contempt of majestic people. (Ps. 123:3–4 FT)

Sitting beside a blind Christian, slowing down to see what he sees of God, offers us an invitation to repent of the arrogance of able-bodiedness and to begin to consider that there might be more for us to learn of the magnificent breadth of the works of the redeeming God of Israel.

The Jesus with Hands

Having learned so much about what is going on in the healing narratives from John Hull, let's allow his sightless experience to lead us into passages we might never have paid attention to as sighted readers.

As a person who lives in a world of touch and hearing, Hull finds three moments in the Gospels exquisitely beautiful. The first is when Jesus responds to the request of a blind man with a pregnant touch. "He took the blind man by the hand and led him outside the village" (Mark 8:23). What must it have been like to be taken by the hand by Jesus? A beautiful gesture of support and intimacy.[23] How might an imaginative engagement with this detail of the story help Christians today feel more intimately what it is like to be with Jesus?

A second moment comes from the Bartimaeus story. When Jesus heard Bartimaeus, "Jesus stood still" (Mark 10:49 KJV). As when he is touched by the woman with the hemorrhage, even amid the babbling and jostling of a crowd, Jesus is finely attuned to the voice and even the touch that cries out for him, the spoken or unspoken call for mercy.[24] Jesus is arrested by and turns his attention to the calling to him of people with disabilities.

A third beautiful moment springs from the implications of the so-called messianic secret.[25] After Jesus heals two blind men in Matthew (9:27–31), he says to them, "See that no one knows about this" (9:30). The striking thing about this command is its impossibility. The ways that blind and sighted people move through space is immediately visible to anyone in the vicinity. Even if the two blind men kept their mouths firmly shut, their every movement and gesture would be a shouted announcement that they had been fundamentally changed.

These three observations are examples of the richness of attention to the actual text of Scripture that follows if we listen to Christians with various disabilities and impairments and to what they pick up in the text.

Instead of going to disabled people armed with a narrow set of texts that seem to mention a given medical condition, what is promising is instead to allow them to take us in new ways to passages in Scripture that we have never previously considered. More specifically, because he is blind, Hull has become especially attuned to moments in Scripture when nonverbal modes of communication, as well as bodily senses other than the eyes, are foregrounded.

Communication beyond Words

Because contemporary Christians inhabit a highly verbal culture, we often do not notice how rich the Bible is in its depictions of nonverbal communication. Those with the experience of living in community with nonverbal people or with those with intellectual difficulties quickly learn how much can be said without words. Christians must learn to pay better attention to the nonverbal communicative realm if we are to love people who cannot speak.[26]

People's bodily posture and movement often matter in biblical stories, as well as their facial expressions, their hand gestures, the way they are said to position their head, and what they are doing as they are speaking. There are even some passages of Scripture that we cannot understand without thinking about the gestures being indicated:

> Whoever winks with their eye is plotting perversity;
>   whoever purses their lips is bent on evil. (Prov. 16:30)

The point in this passage from Proverbs is probably that one can lie without speaking words, something that a blind or deaf person would immediately recognize.

These are only a few aspects of human relations to which the biblical writers are often attentive. They notice nuances of action and feeling that nondisabled readers very often miss and need disabled readers to help us appreciate.[27]

Earlier I made the bold claim that Jesus never heals someone who does not cry out to him. This claim makes sense only if we take bodily communication into account.

Take the woman with the issue of blood in Mark 5:25–34. She does not cry out at all. "When she heard about Jesus, she came behind Him in the crowd and touched His garment. For she said, 'If only I may touch His clothes, I shall be made well.' Immediately the fountain of her blood was dried up, and she felt in her body that she was healed of the affliction" (Mark 5:27–29 NKJV). This woman who has been porously leaking blood for twelve years knows from bitter experience that no doctor can cure her. Yet she has faith that the messiah can. She does not cry out verbally for healing but through the gesture of a touch.

Jesus could feel that a touch as a cry to the messiah was different from the jostling of the crowd. The humor of this tale is that the disciples cannot. When Jesus says, "Who touched me?" they are incredulous: "Look at this crowd, we're all touching you." Jesus can tell the difference between being bumped and a touch of faith. For him a touch in faith is indistinguishable from the verbal cry of need.

There is another telling aspect of this story for a disability reading. We have said that Jesus experiences being blinded and disabled on the cross, and in undergoing this disablement he paradoxically fulfills the law that says no blinded or disabled person should be a priest. A similar inversion of the law's prohibitions happens in the following story. Leviticus 15:7, 11 and Numbers 5:1–5 explicitly call a woman unclean who is menstruating or has any issue of blood. The underlying assumption is that the good boundaries God has given creatures are thrown into question by the periodic leakage undergone by women. This view was shared widely across the ancient world, not only in Israel but also in Greek and Roman cultures. Men are dry, upright, bounded, and self-controlled, and women are wet, soft, emotionally volatile, and leaky. (We will discuss how best to understand the goodness of creaturely boundaries and limits in the next chapter.)

The woman who touches Jesus is thus both physically disabled, in having a long-term illness that severely compromises her body, and also banned from the life of the worshiping community. This has lasted for a dozen years. She reaches out to Jesus in faith that he will liberate her from this long captivity.

A remarkable thing happens next. At her touch in faith, Jesus becomes leaky. She reveals his porosity. Something is going out of him, but he does not know in which direction it has gone, as Candida Moss points out: "In the narrative, the flow of power from Jesus mirrors the flow of blood from the woman. Like the woman, Jesus is unable to control the flow that emanates from his body. Like the flow of blood, the flow of power is something embodied and physical; just as the woman feels the flow of blood dry up, so Jesus feels—physically—the flow of power leave his body. Both the diseased woman with the flow of blood and the divine protagonist of Mark are porous, leaky creatures."[28]

Whereas the law calls leakiness unclean, Jesus reverses the dynamics of contamination. While the law calls for a woman on her period to treat everything she touches as contaminated and unclean, Jesus's leaky body makes everyone who touches it in faith clean. A woman is healed who has been physically disabled for twelve years by what is literally translated as her "fountain of blood." The ceremonial uncleanliness the law attributes to the menses has thus lasted for a dozen long years. The wordless touch in faith by this woman reveals the messiah's leakiness. In healing her, Jesus's porosity has inverted the logic of the law.

This is just one of many more stories that come alive when read by disabled readers. One thing this story highlights is that modern Christians often do not attend sufficiently to the role of touch and gesture in the Bible. Even what we think we know about sight might be misleading us as we read Scripture. The parable of the Good Samaritan, for instance, pivots on the line "when he saw him, he was moved in his bowels" (Luke 10:33 author's trans.).

I recounted in chapter 1 how my experience of disablement provoked by my finger caused me to physically recoil at the sight of a thug breaking another man's hand on television. Jesus's story works the same way, presenting us with a Samaritan whose body reacts immediately and spontaneously to the sight of a suffering human. The loss of certain bodily functions often gives people with disabilities a greater awareness of other types of sensory processes. Jesus presents us with a man, a Samaritan, whose exemplary trait is the capacity to viscerally sense the mortal need of a specific, nearby neighbor.

The Hebraism translated into Greek used here, *splanchnizesthai* ("to be deeply moved" as in "deeply in the bowels"[29]), appears at several crucial points in the Gospels. A depth of bodily connection between human beings is powerfully evoked.

Jesus is depicting the inner dynamics of human life that have been made sensitive to the movements of divine mercy. In Jesus we witness a "self," an embodied identity, who viscerally feels the call to become a servant of God's mercy toward a human being in need of rescue.

Though this mercy is fully embodied only in Jesus, in his parables he nevertheless insists that human works that are pleasing to God are those that join his works of divine mercy. The dis-ease experienced by the Samaritan before the body of the wounded man now appears not as a problem but a gift, an invitation to step into our truest selves by stepping into the gratuitous love of Christ.[30] That gift is not an opportunity to "do something nice," to discharge a merit-building act of charity, but a gratuitous response to God's mercy *to us*.

The Christian's response to the neighbor is called forth because in the neighbor the mercy of Christ calls out: "Truly I tell you, whatever you did for one of the least of these brothers and sisters of mine, you did for me" (Matt. 25:40).

But notice what is entailed in the case of the Samaritan and the beaten man in the ditch. After all, the neighbor in the ditch, who is near unto death, would have been unlikely to have raised his voice— the comportment of his body would have been his call.

Jesus holds the Samaritan up for emulation by Christians for his God-attuned capacity to read the body as a whole, to perceive the rhythms of bodily tension and relaxation, and with them the joy and pain that are characteristic of unique individuals. To recognize the reality of our neighbors as subjects of God's merciful love is, for the Christian, a welcoming of divine mercy poured out on creation by becoming attuned to the physical concreteness and gift-nature of the claim their lives levy. This formed perception must be repentantly received and followed up with a disciplined response that extends over time.

To anticipate chapter 5 on the practicalities of Christian ministry, it is worth noticing here that the Samaritan's next step, after caring solicitously for the beaten man's wounds, is to take him to an inn. He decides to employ what resources he has to procure good quality care for the man. This decision also shows that he recognizes his limits and seeks out the more developed, caring infrastructure available at the inn.

Disabled people rarely want to be pitied (as some versions translate the Samaritan's first glance). They do, however, crave good quality, reliable support. The Samaritan, recognizing this, in essence admits that he is not capable of supporting the man well while he is traveling.

A disability reading also brings about another aspect of the story that is sometimes obliquely noticed but not given its full weight.

Samaritans are ones looked down on by Jews, who considered them much further down in the religious pecking order. As such a "low caste" person, the Samaritan is used to being looked at askance, to being talked down to. Instead of these disparaging glances leading him to try harder to conform to how others think he should act (such as prudently staying away from beaten people on a road known for its robberies), his status as an outsider who is constantly looked down upon seems to embolden him to do what he *should* do in God's sight, no matter the views of those looking down on him.

Jesus seems to have chosen the Samaritan as the exemplar of Christian action in this story because the Samaritan had been freed by constantly living under the disparaging gaze of others to happily defy social convention on behalf of others. This is just one of the ways that those who are "looked down upon" make it easier to see the dynamics of divine mercy in our world. In so doing they offer a provocative challenge to a church passing by on the other side.

Final Words on Jesus and Disability

Christians are followers of Jesus. It is therefore appropriate to have spent a disproportionate amount of time coming to grips with how Jesus can be understood in relation to contemporary ideas about disability.

There is more in the Bible than the four Gospels, however, and the time has come to move further afield to see what the rest of the Bible might have to say about faithfully relating to disability as church today. There is no way to avoid this further work if we want to surmount the problem of having a too-narrow view of the stories of disability in Scripture, as the early sections of this chapter highlighted. People living the disability experience are, like all people, not reducible to their bodily conditions. Their story with God is necessarily more than their disability.

There is an important point here about the Bible as a whole as well. Yes, a lot of people are healed by Jesus in the Gospels, but the Gospels represent the maximal drawing close of God to his people. God's healing and miraculous action comes faster and more furiously at this pinnacle of the biblical narrative, as biblical scholar Grant

Macaskill points out: "In relation to healing in general, it needs to be noted that the stories of healing, as with those concerning exorcism, are particularly clustered within the Gospels and Acts, where they continue to have an exceptional significance. The miracles of Jesus continued to be 'miraculous' and not commonplace; they are exceptional interventions rather than the norm."[31]

That they are not the norm becomes obvious when we look outside of Acts and the Gospels. The wider biblical story of God's journeying with God's people is replete with people who are not healed, even though they are cherished by God and used for his purposes. To overlook this is to fail to do justice to Scripture as a whole, in which the Gospels appear as both continuous with what God has done with God's people and also exceptional and exceptionally new.

Before moving out from Jesus to examine the rest of Scripture, we do well to summarize what close attention to Jesus has taught us about the expectation that "Jesus heals everyone he meets." Even at the pool of Siloam, where Jesus heals the man who cannot get into the pool, he ignores everyone else. This ignoring of everyone who does not cry out to Jesus hints that we should expect the rest of the Bible to challenge our contemporary assumptions about disability.

Fox will help us round this chapter off by summarizing in seven usefully pithy points what Christians today might learn from a disability-sensitive reading of the healings of Jesus.[32]

First, when Jesus engages someone and heals them, the ones who end up healed always go away with a positive view of Jesus. This seems to flatly rule out any healing practices by the church that people experience as unwelcome, embarrassing, or hurtful.

Second, Jesus cares about bodies and about bodily suffering. It is not all he cares about, but his healings are not just social alterations or "all in the mind." Jesus does heal bodies, and not as isolated organ systems but as part of a wider network of relationships that are always also remade. In this light, churches today who simply seek to heal individual bodies without any concern for the networks of rejection and oppression that harm disabled people are not following in the footsteps of Jesus.

Third, Jesus is physically and attitudinally present to the people he heals. He is attentive and compassionate. He listens. Churches today will never be conduits of Jesus's healing if disabled people are not physically present, and if when they are, they are ignored or not listened to compassionately and attentively.

Fourth, the Gospel writers often remark on the impact of the healings on everyone who witnesses them. Churches who are seeking to follow Christ and be a conduit of his healing should be transparently ones in which the onlooking world's injustice is exposed and confronted. Jesus's healings are never solely about the individual. They are always part of Jesus's work of claiming the whole world for a different way of life. It is not the Bible but the influence of biomedical frameworks that focuses modern Christians' expectations of healing solely on making individual body parts normal.

Fifth, most of Jesus's healings display more luminously the true identity of both Jesus *and* the ones who are healed. Jesus reveals that the blind person or the leper is really best understood as a disciple of Jesus. Thus in Jesus's act of healing, he is better understood as the messiah. Churches that seek to follow a healing Jesus today should expect to experience a healing of the busyness and self-absorption that make people with disabilities invisible to congregants. They should also be discovering the unity of the body of Christ across all kinds of functional and cultural differences. Churches that have been given new eyes to see will, for instance, discover in very practical ways how to cross barriers between "leaders" and those our society considers unable to lead or be inside central leadership circles.

Sixth, Jesus's healings always work on multiple levels. Unlike the modern medical practitioner, Jesus never ignores the context in which healing is needed. A church that follows this Jesus will find itself holistically concerned with people's lives, not only seeking to serve and ameliorate their practical pains and dilemmas but also drawing them into a deeper faith and commitment to Jesus.

Finally, Jesus often refuses people's assumptions about disability. To those who ask for mercy he gives mercy—but also healing. To those who think that disability comes from sin, he denies the premise. Jesus never allows the expectations of the age to stand, never leaves people stuck in cycles of thinking and behavior that are not life giving. Churches today that are following the path opened by the healings of Jesus will be places where boundary-bursting practices and ways of thinking are displacing old and tired assumptions and practices that make disabled people feel unwelcome. Churches that seek to follow a healing Jesus today should expect to experience a cleansing of everything that works to marginalize people with disabilities in their church. Our churches need the very cleansing that Jesus extended to lepers.

The story of Tim and Rachel Wright (here told by Tim) echoes many of the biblical themes discussed in this chapter as well as the experiences of Damon Rose and the undesired prayers for his healing that he experienced from Christians. It helpfully clarifies what is at stake in becoming a Jesus-like, healing church and why it demands a transformation of the Christian's—and the church's—self-understanding.

> We stopped asking for Sam to be physically healed as we crossed a watershed of our own, partly due to feelings of loss, defeat and fatigue, but also because we had heard from God, loud and clear. He was saying "no", but over time we came to realize He was not saying "no" to healing, just "no" to our *kind* of healing. We had to learn a whole new type of healing to be praying for; healing which was much more in line with God's priorities. The shock was that the healing had to take place in us, not Sam.
>
> Sam has been the victim of a number of "drive-by prayers" while enjoying a stroll in his wheelchair. "Drive-by prayer" is the phrase we have coined to describe the experience of having a complete stranger, suddenly and without invitation, coming up to Sam, seeing that he is confined to a wheelchair, and spontaneously praying for him.
>
> The last time this phenomenon occurred was during a visit to Salisbury cathedral. We were wandering around as a family, amazed by our surroundings. I was getting to grips with the history of the building and Rachel was soaking up the spirituality of the place (as usual). We were then spotted by a member of the clergy. Dressed in robes that signified her station, she suddenly approached and offered to pray for Sam. I was shocked enough to simply say "yes" so she prayed and then went, leaving me a little bewildered.
>
> As Rachel and I tried to untangle our feelings after the clergy-woman had left, we realized that something was amiss. The very well-intentioned prayer had been entirely focused on Sam's physical appearance: a clearly disabled child in a wheelchair. However, in reality it was Rachel and I who needed prayer, and much more than Sam.

She had focused on the outside, when God looks at the heart. Despite Sam's physical appearance he is very much spiritually whole, whereas I usually find myself in varying levels of spiritual brokenness.

If Sam is visiting a hospital, it would be understandable for a doctor to ask what they can do for him. As a doctor, I strive to help people with their physical or mental health, but have to admit I leave their spiritual needs largely unattended. But in a church situation, Sam is quite possibly the least needy person in the community or building. Sam has less work required on his soul to be more like Jesus than everyone else.

Surely healing from God's perspective is a bigger thing than our physical preconceptions of what looks or feels good; bigger than just postponing death for a few more years, or improving our sporting ability or our appearance, or our ability to pass exams. Not to belittle these very important things. If we employ a much deeper, kingdom-value-based view of healing, we might see healing as a spiritual trans-formation of our understanding of what is making us "sick", taking this one step further: what if our physical or mental suffering is actu-ally leading to our spiritual healing? And if God prioritizes spiritual healing over physical, what are we expecting Him to do?[33]

THREE

God Chose You Because
He Knew You Could Handle It

It is never easy to find the right words to say to people who are going through a difficult time in their lives. Sometimes Christians try to compliment another Christian's strength and patience, or at least the endurance that often grows in people dealing with the disability experience. As one family puts it, "Every special-needs parent I've spoken with has heard, 'I couldn't do what you're doing. You are such special people. God chose you because he knew you could handle it.' We've heard this more times than we care to remember, and we always bristle at the statement."[1] "Bristle" is the polite word for the dark power that misguided attempts to console can have over those who are struggling.[2] Through their very attempts to comfort, friends and loved ones can unleash a crushing sense of isolation and loneliness, observes Rachel Wright: "Although spoken with the best intentions, their platitudes were flimsy and weak, unable to take the weight of our heartache. Like the glare of the hospital lights when we stumbled in from the cold, dark streets, these words made us wince, deepening a sense of isolation and the desire to retreat. The idea that God had singled me out to walk this road less travelled also heightened my sense of loneliness."[3]

God has been good enough to give us a biblical example of such interchanges between believers. Job has some friends who present the world as ordered, just, and rational, in which people get what they deserve. Eliphaz, Bildad, and Zophar try to convince Job that his own bodily suffering and his grief at lost family and social status are both signs of God's justice at work.

Job, however, resists this pastoral advice as misguided. Christians facing a disability experience should likewise feel free to call out as misguided comfort any suggestion that "God knew you could handle it."

Job never really finds out why the hard times in his life have unfolded. And he loudly protests them to God. God hears both Job's protests and the misguided advice given by his friends. God's verdict is clear: "The LORD accepted Job's prayer" (Job 42:9).

Christians wrestling with the disability experience may never learn what it was all about. The book of Job, however, encourages them to make their protest to God and not to accept the superficial explanation that their suffering is somehow fitting or just.

Job leaves us with a final surprise that is as important as it is little noticed. Job's body is never healed of his painful skin condition. One of the most memorable scenes in Job's sufferings is the picture of him scraping his oozing skin lesions with a shard of pottery as he sits beside the fire. And as we saw in chapter 2, in Israel skin disease is associated with the problem of religious exclusion (see Lev. 13 for the details of this prescription).

In the course of the dialogues with his friends, Job often speaks of the challenging and painful nature of his skin condition. Job sees it as an unwarranted evil that has befallen him. His friends see it as a proof that Job has sinned. Yet when Job's property and family are restored in the narrative ending of the book, there is no hint of his skin being restored to health. "God's silence regarding the skin diseases in the epilogue undermines the friends' repeated connection between disease and wrongdoing in the dialogues," suggests Jeremy Schipper.[4] God clearly vindicates Job's character and righteousness but appears not to fully heal him. His worthiness is not dependent on his physical wholeness.

The book of Job robustly resists all suggestions that disability is a matter of some kind of verdict of divine justice. It also rejects any suggestion that someone with a disability cannot be fully worthy, righteous, and favored by God.

There's Bible beyond the Gospels

The truth is, if Christians today think about disability at all, they don't think very far beyond the healing stories of the Gospels. In chapter 2 we went through the stories in the Gospels and let the insights of disabled readers teach Christians today to pick up more of what is going on in the healings of Jesus. Doing so also forced us to clarify several issues of how and why we would do this in dialogue with disability experiences.

The theme of healing forced us to do what academics call hermeneutic work because modern healing is so different from ancient healing that it is very easy to misread the Bible by projecting our contemporary assumptions back onto it. This problem is especially damaging around the figure of Jesus, who, for entirely appropriate reasons, fundamentally shapes the Christian view of the world.

Having done that work in chapter 2, we can now range through the rest of the Bible with the set of insights and lenses that we developed as we wrestled with the Gospel stories. Chapter 2 did not simply catalog all the examples of disabled people in the Gospels, however. We asked instead a slightly different question: How are the biblical writers accepting and challenging the views of disability that were common in their time and place?

One of the basic premises of the Gospel writers is that the figure of Jesus is only intelligible as a work of Israel's God within the framework of Israel's expectations of a messiah. The messiah could be recognized in bringing God's healing, liberation, and restoration to all of creation. It is in the Old Testament where God's desire for the flourishing of all creation is first so richly articulated. And in the New Testament books that follow the Gospels and Acts, we get to see the followers of Christ working to integrate the story of Israel's messiah with what they had seen in the ministry, death, and resurrection of Jesus.

Remember that disability as we know it is a very recent invention. In the ancient world, social support networks were organized around the family unit, and some conditions, such as leprosy, were seen as so contagious that even this support was withdrawn. The leper's physical pain was thus compounded by the extremity of social expulsion. Much to modern disabled people's frustration, some of these exclusionary practices were also religiously sanctioned. This is why the man with leprosy in Mark 1 asks Jesus to be "made clean"—he wants the religious sanction to be lifted.

At this point people with disabilities rightly ask: How could a loving God exclude people, who he has made, just for having some illness or disability? It seems unjust that such sanctions were ever put in place and religiously valorized in Israel. What are we to make of this offense? How should we respond to such texts today?

These themes will be taken up in this chapter, which will first engage some of the relevant passages in the Old Testament in a roughly canonical order. The last section of the chapter will jump back into the New Testament, which depicts Christians as they internalize the new view of the way of life of the people of God that they glimpse in the coming of Israel's messiah.

Genesis and the Goodness of Limits

Reading the Genesis creation accounts having attended to disability experiences reveals the care that God lavishes on all bodies in the creation accounts, especially the human body. God loves and cares for embodied beings.

This love is expressed in the creation accounts by the carefulness of God in giving bodies the defined boundedness they need to be discrete entities. In the creation accounts, to not be formless but to have embodied limits is a marvelous gift. Each created thing is given its own form and discreteness to keep it from dissipating into mixedupness and even total dispersal.

The limits of creatures are not presented as negative in these opening chapters of Genesis. Disability theologians have seen in these opening chapters a crucial theological distinction. Having our own defined and particular limits is good, very good.

"*Dis*ability" is a term that highlights what people cannot do. As Deborah Creamer points out, this is also typically true of the language of limits: "In common usage, the word 'limited' comes with a particular connotation, signifying a lack or absence and emphasizing what cannot be done. It highlights barriers and constraints—one *is* limited." But from the beginning of the Bible, a different perspective is opened up on human life in all its bodiliness: "It emphasizes a characteristic of humanity—one *has* limits. . . . Limits, rather than being an array of unfortunate alternatives to omnipotence, are an unsurprising characteristic of human nature."[5] Having limits is therefore good. It is essential to the creaturely condition. With limits also comes vulnerability. Having limits means humans need things they do not have, like food, and are subject to change. Only God is unchanging. To be a creature is ultimately to cease to function and to die.

From a disability perspective, several things are striking about the biblical creation account.

First, the presentation of the goodness of limited creatures proceeds in a way that does not idealize bodily perfection. The creation stories never dwell on the visible beauty of individual creatures but instead dwell on the beauty of their place within the ecology of God's good working.

Second, this theme of the vulnerability and limitation of the creature as good means we can speak about creatures who have unfamiliar forms without reference to the fall. Difference of form is not a problem for mortal creatures. The creation account assures us that having a form is good. Every creature has to come to terms with their given form and limitations and in this must learn to hear God's pronouncement over what God has created: "It was very good" (Gen. 1:31). This is true of everything God creates.

Third, the second creation account in Genesis 2 highlights God's personal, solicitous concern with, and high valuation of, *every* human body: "Then the Lord God formed a human from the dust of the ground and breathed into his nostrils the breath of life, and the man became a living being" (2:7).

This image of God lovingly creating the human by hand and giving breath through a life-giving kiss is echoed by the psalmist in Psalm 139:13–15.

> For you created my inmost being;
>> you knit me together in my mother's womb.
> I praise you because I am fearfully and wonderfully made;
>> your works are wonderful,
>> I know that full well.
> My frame was not hidden from you
>> when I was made in the secret place,
>> when I was woven together in the depths of the earth.

The writers of Genesis depict the forming of human beings in terms of a potter forming a vessel, while the psalmist depicts it as the work of a divine weaver making a basket. What both images emphasize is that the one who worships this God is one who is learning to receive their body, whatever its form, as lovingly crafted by their maker, by hand.

None of us have the bodies we have because of the random working of evolutionary accidents or even because of the sin and sloth of other human beings. These are only the secondary mechanisms by which God gives each of our lives its form.

The Old Testament is of one voice in saying that God is the agent who has made us and that our having a body with all its limits is an unmitigated good. We have seen how liberating this thought is for many disabled people. It bypasses paralyzing questions about why God has given some people bodies they don't like or that cause them pain. These are questions that can be asked only by people who have been given bodies, and the creation account flatly asserts that the only place to begin to ask such questions is from the initial affirmation that to have been created at all is good.

Fourth, though it may surprise the contemporary reader who tends to see independence as the supreme value, even God appears to create because God is a community and wants to extend community (Gen. 1:26–27). God creates a human, who is then split into man and woman, again, to our surprise, by a process that leaves a wound (2:21–23).

That Eve is born from Adam's side hints at what is to come: a church that is born ever anew from the wound in the crucified Christ's side. Our limits point not only to our vulnerability to being wounded but to the capacity of our wounds to bind us together. In this way the creation story emphasizes the reality of human interdependence as well as our need for community. It also sets the stage for the story to come by highlighting the power of God's desire for communion with us.

In short, the interdependence of creatures *depends* on their being limited and bounded. Having limits and a particular body is not a product of the fall but an original feature of a good creation designed for communion.

Job the Monster, Jacob the Wrestler

The way that the book of Job presents the great monsters of the deep elaborates the creation account's view of the goodness of limits—even in the case of unexpected bodies.

In the climactic scene of the book when God defends himself against the accusations of Job, he lifts up the behemoth and leviathan as examples of creatures who display the majesty of his powerful works (Job 40:15–41:26). In the ancient world these were creatures considered suspect, even evil, because they inhabited the darkest nether regions of the ocean. They were loathed, feared, and scorned in equal parts.

God, however, presents these creatures to Job as examples of the gracefulness and splendor of his creative works. The writer of Job thus directly challenges the marginalizing stereotypes within which these creatures were commonly perceived at the time. God belligerently asserts the beauty of everything he has made, in the face of all detractors. Of leviathan, he insists,

> Can you catch him with a fish-hook
> or run a line round his tongue? (Job 40:25 Jerusalem Bible)

> Any hopes you might have would prove vain,
> for the mere sight of him would stagger you.
> . . . .
> Next I will talk of his limbs
> and describe his matchless strength. (41:1, 4 Jerusalem
> Bible)

You might find leviathan repulsive, says God, but I consider leviathan a masterwork.

This is relevant for our thinking about disability because earlier in the book Job has drawn on this disparaging imagery about leviathan by likening his scaly skin condition to that of a "monster of the deep" (7:12). This sheds a whole new light on the theme of disability. God insists that bodily states that are commonly experienced as monstrous and threatening are not only precious to God but very close to the heart of God's redemptive purposes. The scaly Job, like the scaly leviathan, is not, in fact, a being who lives in the outer margins of life as judged by the normal and healthy (41:15–17). The scaly ones that the normal and healthy fear are being drawn together as residing in the most striking way at the center of God's concern.

Here God's story with the world appears in an especially dramatic form. God's claiming and being with these creatures, precisely because they inhabit bodies that most people find frightful, stands out as something that shatters the presumption of those who are secure in what they take to be their strength and normalcy.[6]

The importance of these themes is highlighted in one of the pivotal stories in Genesis, the story of Jacob wrestling at the Jabbok (32:24–32). Jacob is attacked in his sleep by "a man" with whom he wrestles all night. As they fight, Jacob does not know whether or not he will be killed. But as the night progresses, he realizes he is wrestling not with a man but with God. Jacob demands a blessing.

This is a seminal story in the formation of Israel's identity. Jacob is given a blessing—he is renamed "Israel," one who wrestles with God. Forevermore Israel's children will be known as those who wrestle with God.

In this wrestling match, Jacob's hip is put out of joint. He seems never to fully recover from this injury, and the text tells us that he is left with a lifelong limp. In our terms, he has been disabled. But because this limp was the result of a wondrous wounding in a struggle with God, Israel celebrates it as a sign of divine *favor*, not weakness. The story concludes, "That's why the Israelites don't eat the thigh muscle that's on the hip socket until this day, because he touched Jacob at the hip socket, at the thigh muscle" (Gen. 32:32 FT).

Jacob has been wounded through his struggle in the flesh, but this struggle in the flesh is intertwined with the God who is beyond flesh and blood. This is always the nature of the disability experience. We wrestle with and in our bodies with the God who has made us as we are. Jacob's example teaches us to ask in this wrestling—as painful and bewildering and even life-threatening as it is.

In sum, Jacob's given body was good. And his life with God and his neighbors was also good. In the course of all these relations he was wounded, his struggle with God leaving him with a loss of functionality in his body. The acceptance of a disabled man is celebrated by Israelites down to the present day, for whom this wounding marks the source of their blessed name. In Amos Yong's words, "Jacob's disability serves as a reminder of Israel's covenant relation with God. The limp is not demeaning or emasculating, but a *mark of status*."[7] Whether we say that Jacob's limp is a mark of status or of blessing or of favor or glory, what is clear is that this limp does not make him less in the eyes of the people of God—it makes him *more*.

Mephibosheth's Visible Ankles and Samson's Invisible Hair

The surprising wrinkles a disability reading reveals in some of the founding stories of the Old Testament also turn up in fascinating ways in familiar and unfamiliar Old Testament tales. One less-often-told story is that of the grandson of Saul, Mephibosheth (2 Sam. 4:4; 9:1–13; 16:1–4; 19:24–30; 21:7). For a contemporary reader, Mephibosheth's backstory looks uncomfortably like a story that positions him as a disabled figure who embodies a morally misshapen soul.

Saul, the king chosen because he is beautiful to look upon and taller than all the other Israelite men, has degenerated into an unfaithful king. His family has also fallen into self-destructive infighting. In the course of this infighting one usurping son is pursuing another, and in the tumult of fleeing for her life, the nurse for one of Saul's youngest grandchildren falls, breaking the infant Mephibosheth's ankles. Mephibosheth must now live as the physical embodiment of the divine rejection of Saul's line. Even the name literally means "one who has emerged from shame."[8]

Saul had once embodied the ideal of Hebrew bodily perfection, with the strong ankles associated in the Old Testament with the capacity to stride forth in a commanding way (2 Sam. 2:18; 22:34; Ps. 147:10). He will be followed by a grandson who is a cripple, devoid of these bodily attractions. Furthermore, a new and also physically desirable king is on the rise, David (even if he appears on the scene as the runt of his father's litter [1 Sam. 16:7–11]).

A close reading of the Mephibosheth narrative leaves the reader with the uncomfortable sense that Mephibosheth's disabilities are being highlighted in order to contrast the "unfitness" of Saul's kingly line with the alternative offered in the ruddy and attractive David (1 Sam. 16:12). A disability reading, however, asks us to think about this story from a different angle. It does not erase the discomfort of using a disabled body as a physical representation of a morally and religiously disgraced king. What it does is raise the question of why this story is here in the first place.

The sheer fact that the episode is not expunged from Israel's narrative of its history should tell us something, observes Amos Yong. It "suggests the impossibility of forging disability-free identities, whether in the interpersonal, social or political domains."[9] This story remains in the Bible because Israel does not want to forget that disabled people are part of its own story, its truth. That Mephibosheth remains in the mainstream of God's canonical story with humanity means that those who hear it cannot simply equate disability with rejection by God.

Mephibosheth, remember, is honored by David as the grandson of Saul, the king anointed by God. David himself never equates Mephibosheth's disabilities with divine rejection, troubling the apparently simple equation set up in the story between physical fitness and right to rule.

David, Israel's paradigmatic chosen king, honors the disabled grandson of Saul whose existence is from the beginning associated with Saul's shame, despite the fact that Saul has tried multiple times to kill David: "David said to him, 'Don't be afraid, because I will certainly extend kindness to you for the sake of Jonathan your father. I will give back to you all the land that belonged to your grandfather Saul, and you will be a regular guest at my table'" (2 Sam. 9:7 NET).

God's new and physically attractive king is presented to us as being faithful to God in remaining true to the legacy of his divinely appointed predecessor. Mephibosheth remains present with David in the unsettling form of a life that seems tragic and compromised—but not removed from God's story with Israel.

The similarly unsettling ending of Samson's story (Judg. 16) includes a humorous twist that is very illuminating from a disability perspective. In ancient thought, blindness was often linked to spiritual insight, a connection that we saw in some of the stories of Jesus healing blind people in the Gospels. The Samson story approaches this theme from the perspective of a man who is blinded by being able to see. Samson's sight is his fatal point of spiritual temptation and weakness.

Ancient people thought of their eyes as projecting rays out into the world, reaching out and grabbing images and bringing them back to the eye.[10] Samson is depicted as someone whose roving eye is his downfall. He sees women, he wants them, and he has to have them, even if he has to kill a thousand Philistines to get them. He is finally led by his eyes to desire Delilah, who betrays him.

The first twist in this tale is that it is not the eventual loss of his eyes that disables him but the loss of his hair. Once his hair is shorn, he becomes like every other man (normal!). Once he is rendered less able through the loss of his hair, he is overpowered by soldiers, taken into captivity, and his eyes are gouged out (Judg. 16:19–21). Even if his becoming "normal" did not disable him, being blinded surely does.

Here's what we need to notice: the text refuses at this point to fall into the groove of the ancient trope of blindness as a road to wisdom. It allows no more than that with his loss of eyesight Samson no longer can fall prey to his besetting temptation. In this roundabout way Samson reinters God's purposes for him. Without his eyes, he is forced to wait for God's leading.

At the pinnacle of the story, a disability reading offers a stunning new insight. The Philistines make the usual assumption of sighted people that being blind is a debilitating condition. This is a fatal error. They compound their error by bringing Samson out at a party to make fun of him, standing him between two load-bearing pillars. Samson has never prayed to have his sight back, and he does not do so now. We can also tell that he has not become much wiser through his ordeal because all he prays for is for vengeance for his lost eyes (Judg. 16:28). Even this less-than-inspiring prayer is heard by a gracious God. Samson is allowed to complete his vocation as a judge in Israel and as a warrior against Israel's enemies, with all the compromise and bloodshed that entails. He is embraced as another link in God's story, as messy as his story has been. He is loved and preserved in God's story as a disabled person.[11]

To anticipate the final topic of this chapter, we see in Samson yet another illustration that for God's people, physical integrity is less salvifically relevant than loyalty to God and God's people.

The Law's Painful Exclusions

The creation accounts in Genesis are directly connected to the law in the Old Testament. God makes creatures with limits and distinctions that are good and life giving. A sinful and rebellious humanity ignores the goodness of these limits and strives to overcome them, leading to destructive chaos. The giving of the law is God's way of drawing attention once again to the goodness of given limits and boundaries. In learning the goodness of limits, humans can begin to respect the givenness of creatures.

The passages that people with disabilities find most discomfiting appear in the laws about who can and cannot be a priest and also in the descriptions of disabilities as being given by God as punishments for disobedience (Lev. 21:17–23; Deut. 28:25–29, 58–60). It is important that we not try to evade or soften the offensiveness of these passages for modern ears: "Through their generations, no individual from your offspring in whom there's a defect is to draw near to present his God's meal. Because no individual in whom there's a defect is to draw near: one blind or lame or disfigured or deformed, one who has an injury to his leg or an injury to his hand, or one who is a hunchback or dwarf or defective in his eye or [has] scab or sore or crushed testicle" (Lev. 21:17–20 FT).

There is no doubt that a range of disabilities is being arrayed here in a manner that gives the impression that God sees the disabled people as blemished. This is a very hard passage. It is also a perplexing passage, as we have seen that the patriarch Jacob, who becomes Israel, has an "injury to his leg." How can someone who was the paradigm of the faithful Israelite not be eligible to be a priest in Israel?

One of the most important differences between Christian and Jewish readings of the Old Testament is their reading of the law. This passage is especially impacted by the new relation to the law that Jesus teaches and embodies.

Christian readers have usually taken one of three routes to deal with the challenge of this text.

The first is to say that these are ceremonial laws having to do with worship in Israel. They cannot be fulfilled in Israel because there is no temple to observe them in and because they do not need to be fulfilled, since Jesus proclaims himself the new temple and the final sacrifice in Israel.

A second reading allegorizes these prohibitions as speaking not about physical exclusions from the ministry but about moral exclusions. The passage is not taken as barring people with disabilities from Christian ministry, and it remains relevant for thinking about the negative spiritual qualities that a Christian priest or pastor should not have. This reading embraces the understanding of physical disabilities as symbols of moral or spiritual deficiencies.

The first solution is difficult because it tends to divide the Old Testament into binding and nonbinding parts, and it depends on a church-Israel sequence that tends to see the church as replacing Israel (the supersessionist problem). The second solution has the advantage of seeking some sense in which the passage remains binding Scripture for Christians, but it has the disadvantage of doing so by reinforcing the ancient use of visible physical deformities as symbols of moral deformities. Any such equation remains highly problematic for Christians concerned with disability issues.

It therefore seems best to prefer a third reading, a christological one in which Jesus is understood as the epistle to the Hebrews presents him. Jesus is the perfect priest and the perfect offering. Jesus ends the quest set out in the law for a blemish-free act of worship.

It is worth pausing here to take in this breathtaking move. The law says that no one with this range of disabilities can be priest in Israel. Yet as God unfurls the story of Israel in the New Testament, the perfect priest who fulfills the ceremonial law and so completes it does so hanging from a cross. The Jesus who is wounded and broken for us is, in this particular wounding, breaking, and even blinding, perfectly fulfilling the role of the priest in Israel. Israel honored this priesthood by allowing the most exemplary human beings to inhabit it, but God contradicts this construal of the perfect priest in his very person.

This christological reading is crucial for a theologically satisfactory account of disability. Jesus fulfills the quest for the perfect priest and sacrifice *in an impaired and disabled body*. In so doing God points forward to a corporate body of Christ that will include all sorts of bodies. In the perfect high priest we glimpse in microcosm what is to come, the woundedness and completeness of Christ's corporate body in all its diversity.[12] On the cross we see Jesus as both the member looked up to and honored as well as the less presentable member (more on this shortly).

The Prophets' Unsettling Inclusions

The New Testament's insistence that Jesus was the perfect priest and the unblemished sacrifice thus undermines and unravels normate and ableist stereotypes about the superiority of the blemish-free body to all other bodies. To understand why, we must turn to the prophets.

The prophets offer the key to overturning the normate assumption that perfect bodies are superior to all other bodies. Several passages in Isaiah beautifully welcome the disabled without any hint that they need healing. In Isaiah 42:18–19, blind people are presented as a model of faithfulness, a vision that is paralleled in Jeremiah 31:8–9. Micah presents God as especially eager to gather those who in the course of God's story he has rendered blind and lame for his purposes.

> That day—it is Yahweh who speaks—
> I will finally gather in the lame,
> and bring together those that have been led astray
> and those that have suffered at my hand.

> Out of the lame I will make a remnant,
> and out of the weary a mighty nation.
> Then will Yahweh reign over them
> on the mountain of Zion
> from now and for ever. (Mic. 4:6–7 Jerusalem Bible)

The prophets depict those who have been exiled by the prescriptions of the law as the ones closest to God's heart. As the book of Job links Job as scaly outcast with the scaly and feared leviathan, the God depicted in Scripture apparently enjoys revealing himself in all his glory precisely in those people and creatures whom most people fear and look down on. This is why it is fitting for Isaiah to tell his readers to look for a suffering servant whose "appearance was . . . disfigured" (52:14). The prophets' vision of God's heart for the disabled outcast gives Christians new eyes as they read the law.

As John Hull observes, "God prefers the lame and other people who have been driven out, because in a very special way they symbolize the alienated and oppressed people whom God delights to deliver. We notice also that they are delivered not by being saved from their disabilities, in a series of healing miracles, but by becoming the people of God."[13] The prophets were not just making this stuff up. They found it in the law.

The law plays a starring role in the book of Exodus. Exodus tells the story of the giving of the law, its establishment as the constitution of the covenant people of God. At the heart of this narrative lies the reality that the Israelites were *gerim*, foreigners or resident aliens, while in captivity in Egypt. The narrative of Israel's rescue out of the horror of slavery is unpacked in the law as an ethical imperative: "You must not oppress the stranger [*ger*]; you know how a stranger feels, for you lived as strangers in the land of Egypt" (Exod. 23:9 Jerusalem Bible; cf. 22:21).

Frances Young sees this stranger, this uncanny person who is not-like-us-yet-of-us as "a sign of what Israel truly is, and the 'outsider' prophet a sign of God's otherness, God's strangeness."[14] For Young, people with severe intellectual disabilities can be understood as very similar to the foreign stranger in the Old Testament. The person with intellectual difficulties confronts us as an uncanny person who is not-like-us-yet-of-us. Young highlights how central the problem of being socially marginalized is in the world of the Old Testament.

The Israelites may not have been disabled in Egypt (though it is likely, since starvation and servitude do disable the body), but they were definitely not-like-us-yet-of-us in a manner that God commanded them to remember. God's people must never lose their sensitivities to the discomforts of people who are living at the margins of social acceptability and secure belonging.

That sensitivity to the marginalized is one that converts directly into a sensitivity to those who occupy that not-like-us-yet-of-us position today—the disabled chief among them. Over and over again, readers with a disability experience notice and draw succor from this theme, as Fox found in her research among disabled interpreters of the Gospels.

> Knowing that very often people with serious illness or disability are outcasts in the historical world of the Gospels (with some notable exceptions), [disabled] interpreters notice details in the narratives that highlight this reality. . . . In the healing of the man born blind (Jn 9), neither the community members nor the Pharisees initially believe the man's testimony—an indication of his lack of relationships and social status. Then, though Bartimaeus is the one healed person whose name we know, he is still clearly an outsider, portrayed as marginalized at the side of the road, begging. The man oppressed by demons in Gerasene is an especially strong picture of isolation. . . . Not only does Jesus simply meet him among the tombs, away from the rest of the community, but as the text says, "he 'had a home' there."[15]

As we move from the Old Testament over the continental divide in Scripture that is the Gospels we come down from those lofty heights to the New Testament, where we find the earliest Christians puzzling through the same set of questions that we have observed in the law and the prophets—but having been reoriented by their encounters with Jesus.

Peter Sets a Bad Precedent

Extending the pattern set in the Gospels, the story of the birth of the church told in Acts also opens with a healing (3:1–10). Unfortunately,

Peter and John may not have been paying close enough attention to how Jesus healed. They appear to set a precedent that would valorize some unseemly behavior among Christians in centuries to come. The two apostles are going to the temple when a "man who was [crippled] from birth" asks them for money (3:2). The experiences many disabled people have with Christian faith healers cause them to recoil at the apostles' response. "Peter looked straight at him, as did John. Then Peter said, 'Look at us!' So the man gave them his attention, expecting to get something from them" (3:4–5).

Let's pause here for a moment.

Forget that the story comes out well.

Acts begins with Jesus sending out the disciples to proclaim his name, and they faithfully do so in the first two chapters of Acts. But this story suggests they may not have always gotten things just right. We need to keep in mind all the protests we have heard from people with disabilities. Many tell stories of people approaching them and praying for healing of something that they were not seeking healing for.

Remember that as depicted in the Gospels, Peter especially has not always been an exemplar of perfect discipleship—often precisely the opposite. As the disciples begin their ministry, Peter will continue to blunder along *almost* getting it right, as he has done throughout his tenure with Jesus. This is why we should not necessarily assume that Christians today should copy what sounds like an imperious tone Peter takes up here. Christians follow Jesus, not his witnesses, the often very human apostles.

Roll tape.

"Then Peter said, 'Silver or gold I do not have, but what I do have I give you. In the name of Jesus Christ of Nazareth, walk'" (Acts 3:6). There is definitely good news here. Peter and John don't have the money, and they give a better gift, offering a healing that also reintroduces the man into the community of faith. At the same time they seem to have forgotten how carefully Jesus attended to the requests of people with disabilities.

Peter and John also depart from the pattern Jesus established in his healings (he always responded to someone calling out to him), and they do not listen for someone to call out before they respond with healing. The man is healed when he has not yet turned toward Jesus, only praising Jesus *after* the healing.

Notice also that the text says that the man has been crippled "from birth" and that he begs daily. Recall also that Jesus has been in the temple daily, which is why his disciples continue to meet there after Jesus's ascension. Not only was Jesus in the temple daily, but he was healing there, which is one of the things that most infuriated the temple authorities (Matt. 21:14–15).

The man has been begging at this gate his whole life, and Jesus came to the temple daily. The conclusion is unavoidable: Jesus had almost certainly passed this begging man without healing him, nor had he been asked for healing. Jesus was a known quantity. Everyone in the temple was talking about him. And he was known as a healer.

So we don't really know why Peter decided that this man's time had come for healing. Peter might have been frustrated at the man's resistance to Jesus. Peter might have been emboldened to undertake an impulsive act by the many people who were responding to the message of Jesus. Or he may have been in a place of doubt, needing to reach out and proclaim someone healed, so that when it did not happen, he could give the whole "Jesus thing" up once and for all.

All we know is what he did: he dispensed a healing that had not been asked for, upon someone who knew Jesus and who would have asked himself had he wanted healing.

In not *quite* getting their response right, Peter has put the Holy Spirit of Jesus in a bind. What is Jesus to do? These are his witnesses! Even though Peter has not listened as closely as he should, Jesus nevertheless heals the man through the Spirit, for *his* name's sake. In so doing he leaves it for Christians reading this story for centuries to come to ask whether we can learn from Jesus's example what Peter did wrong.

Roll tape.

"Taking him by the right hand, [Peter] helped him up, and instantly the man's feet and ankles became strong. He jumped to his feet and began to walk. Then he went with them into the temple courts, walking and jumping, and praising God" (Acts 3:7–8).

Okay, maybe Peter has learned a bit from Jesus. The gesture of intimacy in Peter taking the man's right hand certainly echoes what we saw in several of Jesus's healings, as does the subsequent verses' note that the people who saw it were filled with wonder and amazement (Acts 3:9–10). This was not just a healing of one man's body. Rather, it drew a group of people toward the name of Jesus and reintroduced the man into the community of faith. It was probably just as healing for Peter, who almost certainly had not forgotten his own denial of Jesus at the crucifixion.

Here is the bottom line: Jesus is not constrained in his redeeming work by disciples and witnesses who do not get it quite right (thank God). Peter's falling short is a reminder that the shortcomings of the church do not thwart the work of the Holy Spirit. God's capacity to call people to Godself even goes as far as the Gospel writers themselves. In this story the writer of Luke and Acts comes dangerously close to reinscribing the ableist narrative we saw in the Mephibosheth story, in which lameness of ankles stands in for negative spiritual states. What saves this passage from tipping over into the trope of "strong ankles as symbol of a beautiful soul" is that the newly healed body of the man is not presented as strong in itself. The healing of his ankles is immediately turned to the purpose for which every creature is made: jumping up and down in praise of God.[16]

Philip Sets a Good Precedent

I do not think it accidental that the first scene of Peter and John's ministry, with all its complications, is paralleled by the final scene of the first part of Acts. Luke presents a provocative story at the hinge between the curtain dropping on Peter's story and raising on Paul's story, which takes up the second half of the book.

This is the delightful interlude with the apostle Philip and the Ethiopian eunuch (Acts 8:26–40). An angel directs Philip to set out down the road away from Jerusalem. As he is walking down the road, lo and behold, a very powerful representative of Candace, the queen of the Ethiopians, passes by on a chariot. "The Spirit told Philip, 'Go to that chariot and stay near it.' Then Philip ran up to the chariot and heard the man reading Isaiah the prophet" (8:29–30).

Stop motion.

This is glorious comedy. God is literally having an apostle run alongside a man in a chariot and try to strike up a conversation. In the ancient world people did not read silently. So Philip is also eavesdropping. He's the guy who starts reading your newspaper while sitting next to you on the bus. But the comedy has a serious point. Something really special is going on here, if we understand this event within the story of God with Israel.

The man Philip meets is a eunuch, and in the ancient world, eunuchs would have their testicles removed before entering service. Recall that having "damaged testicles" categorically falls foul of the Levitical prohibition (Lev. 21:20; 22:24; Deut. 23:1). The eunuch is not a candidate for the priesthood in Israel, though he is soon to become part of the kingdom of priests that is the Christian church. What is important to notice is that his very role as a castrated courtier publicly displays his having a physical condition that has been labeled a disqualifying blemish in Israel.

Thus we have here a man who, in addition to being a gentile, flagrantly violates two other ancient stereotypes about desirable bodies. It is likely that his skin is black, which in the Mediterranean world was often assumed to be a sign of inferiority. And he has a physical deformity, in being castrated, which would have been visible in his dress and social position. This puts him in a group that was religiously stigmatized in Israel's law.

But he is reading Isaiah, which, as we have seen, emphasizes God's heart for the outcast, and even promises that eunuchs will find fertility and a place in God's story (Isa. 56:4–5). And the Spirit wants him.

The Spirit wants him. We must not underplay the importance of this crucial factor. The man whose body so many would have looked down on, in more than one way, is still wholly desired by God. God so desires this person that he makes the apostle into a fool for Christ, a running-alongside-eavesdropping kind of fool.

And the Spirit catches the eunuch, through the faithfulness of a disciple who does not let his prejudices stand in the way of following God's leading (in this, being a Good Samaritan).

What happens next is all important: "He invited Philip to come up and sit with him" (Acts 8:31).

Have you ever tried to read and have a serious conversation in a moving chariot? If you have ever had the misfortune to ride in any sort of horse-drawn wagon on an unpaved road, you'll know that the obvious thing for Philip to do would have been to ask the Ethiopian to stop. But Philip climbs right up and dives into discussing how Jesus fulfills the expectations of Isaiah. He adjusts his pace to that of the one who the Spirit is after, no matter how uncomfortable it feels at first.

The eunuch believes in Jesus, has the chariot stop by some water, and asks to be baptized.

Philip shows us what it looks like to categorize people not by their bodies but by their desirability to God. Philip shows us what it looks like when the Holy Spirit's desire to join people together overwhelms the human sense of social barriers and awkwardness. Philip shows us what it is like for the disciples to match their pace to the person before them. He is not afraid to jump onto a wheelchair and ride along with the eunuch, without prejudice, to hear the eunuch's questions *from his vantage point.*

The eunuch, too, shows us something about what it means for disabled people to come into the presence of the people of God. He has traveled a very long way and is seeking to join the worship of Israel by reading the Scriptures of a foreign people. Even if he is politically powerful, he is so visibly in a body that some people find odd and even repulsive.

Philip lets the Spirit lead him into the foolishness of chasing and then climbing up to travel alongside this man. To join him in his questioning. Philip does not assume that the Ethiopian wants his body changed. He recognizes in the Ethiopian's questions a searching desire to worship with the people of God. Philip sees this as precious and sees that it is the work of the Holy Spirit.

Every church should be a Philip-church. But how many are? How easily Philip might have missed the Spirit's leading. How easily we as the church fall short of his example.

When it goes wrong, the church spits in the face of those the Spirit is running after, suggests Amy Jacober. In her research she heard the story of one mother of a special needs daughter who had been raised in a church where maturing children either reaffirmed their infant baptism or were baptized for the first time. Her daughter attended the preparation classes with her friends, and then the question arose about whether she would be baptized.

> The church leadership held a meeting, convened a committee, and tasked the pastor with informing the mother of their decision. The pastor said they would be happy to pray for her daughter, but she was not a candidate for baptism because they believed she did not understand the meaning of baptism. This act was so sacred, they rationalized, that baptism itself would be defiled should it be administered to anyone who had less than a full understanding of what was taking place. Baptizing a person with a disability, they argued, would cheapen the sacred duty of the church to administer such a ritual. Through tears she told of her daughter's love for Jesus and of her daughter's insatiable desire to be at church and serve others. Her daughter was understanding of the church's position and wanted to stay at that church, but the mother just could not stay. She still believed in God, but didn't have the theology to figure out what was taking place with her daughter. She hoped that somehow that individual church was screwed up, but she had not, as of that time, found a place that would love her daughter the way she believed God did.[17]

In the next chapter we are going to move on to some of the theological questions raised by disability, such as the problem of understanding how much knowledge it takes to make a good confession, which is what tangled up the church leaders in this story. The truth is that Christians won't be in a place to seriously engage the theological questions involved unless we have been converted into followers like Philip, for whom stigmatized bodies do not even present a bump in the road.

Paul the Sight-Impaired Apostle

Being a blind theologian, John Hull is especially attuned to the use of visual images and metaphors in the Bible. He makes a striking observation about Paul's use of visual language. Paul generally employs metaphors of sight in a much less either-or fashion than do other authors of the Bible. In the Gospel of John, for instance, people are *either* sighted or blind, nothing in between. Paul, in contrast, continually draws on images of foggy mirrors, of blurry vision, and of eyes being scaled over.[18]

In Galatians 4:13–16 Paul also speaks of having a debilitating illness and of his gratitude to the Galatian Christians for not having treated him as disabled people could expect to be treated in the ancient world, with "contempt or scorn" (4:14). Rather, "if you could have done so, you would have torn out your eyes and given them to me" (4:15).

This passage, in combination with the conclusion of Galatians where Paul points out that the proof that he is taking over from his secretary is "what large letters I use as I write to you with my own hand" (6:11), makes it plausible to assume that what he calls the weakness of his flesh or his thorn in the flesh might well have been very bad eyesight. As the disability theologian Amos Yong points out, "Perhaps the closest ancient Greek parallel to the modern term 'disability' is the word *asthenēs* ('weak') and its correlates."[19]

The account of Paul's conversion in Acts 9 fits the unsettling Old Testament trope of people having their sight taken away as a punishment for sin. In Genesis 19:11, Lot's assailants are stricken blind, as are the Egyptians in Exodus 10:21–23, when they will not let the Israelites go. Elisha similarly prays to smite the Arameans blind in 2 Kings 6:18.

What is important to notice is that as Paul is turned around on the Damascus road to become Jesus's servant, the course of his ministry overturns any assumption that weak eyesight has anything to do with moral weakness or spiritual disorientation. In Luke's hands, the idea of the privation of sight as a punishment is morphed into a story of prophetic formation through the removal of one sense. Saul becomes Paul because, unlike Samson, the loss of sight becomes a chance for growth in faith and a deepening of his relationship with God.

More pointedly, Paul considers his being robbed of sight to be an incorporation into Jesus's death. The clue here is that as the light from heaven flashes around him, Paul "fell to the ground," and the voice from heaven tells him to "get up and go" (Acts 9:4, 6). "Saul's sightlessness lasts for three days," notes Adam Booth. "In view of the frequent notices in Luke-Acts that Jesus must be raised 'on the third day' (Luke 9:22; 13:32?; 18:33; 24:7, 46; Acts 10:40), this too may be taken as a parallel."[20] The link between Jesus's death and Paul's losing his old life to be raised up into new life is hammered home in Acts 9:18. After Paul is filled with the Spirit, "something like scales fell from Saul's eyes, and he could see again. He got up and was baptized."

Adam Booth observes that "through an embodied imitation of Jesus's death and resurrection, [Paul] has been made 'like his teacher' (Luke 6:40), encountering what the historical Paul called a 'death like his' (Rom. 6:5)."[21]

The divine removal of Paul's sight once again inverts the negative links set up in the Old Testament between blindness and punishment. Paul is forced to stop killing Christians when his sight is taken away, and he is made into a powerful witness even though his sight barely recovers.

Acts presents us with an account of Paul's blindness displaying how a sensory impairment can become a context for spiritual maturation. The weakening of some of his powers (sight) becomes the divine invitation to allow others to grow (rhetorical, theological, prophetic, missional).

Paul and God's Foolishness

Perhaps because Paul had such a tangible disability experience, it is very easy to find themes of relevance to disability experience in his work. Let's look at a couple from his first letter to the Corinthian church. Paul writes this letter to weigh in on a debate among Christians in Corinth about the shape of the gospel. Some in the church think that the good news of Jesus is best displayed in Christians who look wise and speak persuasively. Others think that the essence of the gospel is displayed in those Christians who possess flashy spiritual gifts. Others think that a true Christian looks like Paul or like Jesus himself.

Paul replies that the way of Jesus is the way of the cross. He stakes his claim right away and without any caveats.

> Has not God made foolish the wisdom of the world? For since in the wisdom of God the world through its wisdom did not know him,

God was pleased through the foolishness of what was preached to save those who believe. Jews demand signs and Greeks look for wisdom, but we preach Christ crucified: a stumbling block to Jews and foolishness to Gentiles, but to those whom God has called, both Jews and Greeks, Christ the power of God and the wisdom of God. For the foolishness of God is wiser than human wisdom, and the weakness of God is stronger than human strength. (1 Cor. 1:20–25)

The debater and the rhetorician were the paragons of worldly intelligence in first-century Greco-Roman culture. By definition, people with disabilities were their opposite, the "weak," with whom we have seen Paul identifying himself.

The term "foolishness" appears five times in 1 Corinthians 1:18–23, despite the fact that the term (literally, "moron") was as pejorative in Paul's time as it remains today. Yet this is precisely the site where Paul keeps insisting that the saving power of the crucified Christ will appear.

Paul also emphasizes that there are different kinds of wisdom. The wisdom that most people want admires the powerful and influential, an elite patrician class. For Paul the cross displays a counter-wisdom found among the foolish.

Given this train of connections, it is hard to imagine that Paul does not have people with all sorts of disabilities in mind, especially those with intellectual disabilities, when he delivers the knockout punch in 1 Corinthians 1:27: "But God chose the foolish things of the world to shame the wise; God chose the weak things of the world to shame the strong." Paul is not just siding with the weak against the strong, though he is doing that. He insists that this is the cosmic reality that is revealed in the work of Jesus Christ, specifically his work on the cross.

The crucified Christ is the supreme symbol of all that was weak and foolish in the Roman world. Famously, the earliest picture of Jesus ever found by archaeologists is a mocking cartoon of a crucified man depicted with the head of an ass.[22] Paul has been so deeply schooled in the stories of Israel that he knows that God raises his children up out of defeat. And on this Paul is all in. He does not try to cover up the shame of a crucified messiah. He draws attention to it.

In our terms, the crucified person is the ultimate dis-abled person, an inhabitant of the most socially stigmatized social location that can be achieved in Roman society.

Yet, as we've discussed, Jesus fulfills the Levitical priesthood not as the perfect and unblemished one but as the one bloodied, wounded, and shamed. With his impaired body he overcomes any hint of disability as a taint that disqualifies one for holiness.

It is this Jesus whom Paul insists on presenting as counter to those Corinthian Christians' vision of a Jesus who is perfect, who is powerful, who is polished and speaks well. "I resolved to know nothing while I was with you except Jesus Christ and him crucified. I came to you in weakness with great fear and trembling. My message and my preaching were not with wise and persuasive words, but with a demonstration of the Spirit's power, so that your faith might not rest on human wisdom, but on God's power" (1 Cor. 2:2–5). In following a Christ who is most powerful in weakness, Paul discovers a new vision of how people in the church are to relate to one another.

Paul as a Good Waiter

In the next chapter we will return to dig deeply into Paul's account of the spiritual gifts in 1 Corinthians 12, but here I want to end this short examination of the disability themes in Paul's work by looking at the amazing conclusion of the discussion that makes up 11:17–34.

This passage engages the practical problems that emerge when the church does not overcome the divisions between people who think of themselves as elite and those who experience life as outsiders or untouchables.

In the first few decades of the Christian movement, churches had no purpose-built buildings in which to meet. The church had to gather in the houses of its rich members, including for worship services.

Rich people in the Roman world had all the usual conventions of elite social gatherings. They knew who was appropriate to invite to a party and who was not. They knew how to keep appropriate distance between those who were being served and those who served them. And they were comfortable getting a little tipsy together with the other more elite members of the community.[23]

Paul is upset with the Corinthians because their worship services have been conforming to the conventions of the rich person's dinner party. They are confusing the relational dynamics that ought to characterize Christian worship in celebration of the work of the crucified Christ with an indulgent meal among elites.

The presenting issue is that the rich patrons are having what they would consider a normal dinner party, while the poor Christians (many of whom were slaves) were coming in at the end after a long day and being given whatever scraps were left over from the fellowship meal that the wealthier Christians had been enjoying for some hours.[24]

For Paul, such behavior makes a mockery of the foolishness of the cross, and he explodes. "When you gather in the same place, you can't possibly be eating the Lord's Supper. Each of you eats his own supper without waiting for each other. So one person goes hungry and another gets drunk. Don't you have homes in which to eat and drink? Do you despise God's church and embarrass people who don't have anything to eat? What can I say to you? Should I praise you? I won't praise you for this" (1 Cor. 11:20–22 GW). Paul is genuinely angry here. His anger is directly linked to the theme of disability, because slavery in the ancient world (as in almost every culture) is disabling. The slave's body is to be used—and used up.

Paul indirectly highlights this connection between slavery and disability when he says in 1 Corinthians 11:30, "That is why many among you are weak and sick, and a number of you have fallen asleep." Paul is not saying that the community is being judged with illness because it is sinning. He is saying that the relational patterns in this church community are sick. Sick patterns of relationships make people sick by robbing other bodies of the strength they need to stay well. Paul is genuinely offended that a thieving form of social order has infected their gathering as church. Those who are getting fat off the labor of others in their daily economic relations do the same when they gather for the Lord's Supper.

To highlight how this insult injures the body of Christ, Paul calls it a humiliation of the weakest (1 Cor. 11:22). Paul has firmly identified himself from the outset of the letter as allied with these weak ones as a follower of a humiliated, crucified Christ.

Paul reiterates that his understanding of church comes from the crucified Christ in the words that now lie at the very heart of Christian worship: "For whenever you eat this bread and drink this cup, you proclaim the Lord's *death* until he comes" (1 Cor. 11:26). When you take communion together, Paul insists, you are proclaiming the one who was humiliated and whose body was publicly broken. Whoever once again humiliates those whose bodies are humiliated and broken "will be guilty of sinning against the body and blood of the Lord" (11:27). This is strong language, but Paul wants to emphasize the deadly seriousness of the problem. Any gospel that thinks the good news of Jesus is all about achieving strength and perfection is despising the very weakness through which God shows his redeeming power. Christians prove they despise weakness in the ways they act toward those they assume to be weak.

The remarkable thing is how simple his proposal is to fix the problem in the Corinthian church. It is so simple that it is tempting to dismiss it as not really serious. But he's deadly serious. In fact, if the church really got Paul's proposal, there would be no tension around disabled people in the church, any church. "So then, my brothers and sisters, when you come together to eat, wait for one another" (1 Cor. 11:33 NRSV). It's hard to believe that this could be Paul's proposed solution. Yet he really seems to mean it when he says that the power of God is shown in weakness. There is no irony in his insistence that he follows a God who became a humiliated outcast to reveal that no one is a humiliated outcast.

Paul's constant emphasis is on having been baptized into Christ's *death*, not his resurrection, his power, or his glory but his death. We are united as Christians in communion in the very mode of God's reaching out to all of us through this moment of God's own brokenness. As Rachel and Tim Wright observe, "Communion is the moment when, as a collective Church, we stand (or sit) together and acknowledge that we are all broken but united in our brokenness. Communion is not simply about fixing our broken pieces; it's about acknowledging that this is the pattern in which God chose to express His love to us: 'broken and given.'"[25] And if you take that seriously, really seriously, Paul proposes you will wait for one another. Those who know themselves as broken, as united in a broken Christ, never rush ahead without the others.

Those who know themselves in the crucified one will not organize their churches around the desires of the eloquent and powerful to have a church configured to serve the eloquent and powerful. Those who know themselves in the crucified one will not organize their churches around the desire to put on a spectacle that will amaze people and draw big crowds. Those who know themselves in the crucified one will be looking out for and embracing people who seem to offer nothing, who appear not to be able to contribute. To do so makes them a community that is continually having to learn what it means to travel at the speed of others so that the bonds of community can flourish.[26]

A church that waits for one another in all these ways will soon discover a whole new world. They will discover what it means to be one body. As they relinquish an understanding of the good news of Jesus as an offer of power, security, and success, Christians begin to understand their intrinsic connections with one another. Thank God for sending a sight-impaired apostle to welcome the outcasts into the body of his holy people.

Disabled at the Heavenly Banquet

The Christian celebration of the Lord's Supper provides the worshiping community with a foretaste of the final eschatological banquet. That is why Paul is so worked up about the malformed celebration going on in Corinth.

Chapter 4 will more explicitly discuss the question of the resurrected body. I will end this chapter's treatment of disability themes in the Bible by returning to the Gospels—specifically, to two of Jesus's parables about the kingdom of heaven.

The first is the parable of the banquet as recounted in Luke 14:7–24. Once again the problem among people that Jesus wants to confront is a vision of the gospel that people think will move them up the social pecking order. Jesus gets at this with a story about people angling to get a more prestigious seat at the dinner table. "Then Jesus said to his host, 'When you give a luncheon or dinner, do not invite your friends, your brothers or sisters, your relatives, or your rich neighbors; if you do, they may invite you back and so you will be repaid. But when you give a banquet, invite the poor, the crippled, the lame, the blind, and you will be blessed. Although they cannot repay you, you will be repaid at the resurrection of the righteous'" (Luke 14:12–14).

Some Christians have taken passages like this as an affirmation that Christians are the ones who should do works of charity for unfortunate people and that God will one day reward them. This is a long and venerable theological tradition within the Christian church. This reading, however, has drawn fire from disability theologians. What has come to be called the "critique of the charity model" resists the urge to draw from this passage a firm distinction between Christians and disabled people. Drawing such a distinction is bad for everyone, Amy Jacober observes: "Too often those with disabilities have been viewed as projects for ministry, not partners in ministry. We have assumed they will be blessed to be a part of someone else's discipleship even if they do not experience the demands and joys of discipleship themselves."[27]

Jesus himself directly challenges a charity-model reading of this story. In the extended version of the story he immediately tells next (Luke 14:15–24), a man invites people to a great banquet, but the "high status" people refuse to come. They give the sort of excuses that people with money and property are wont to have. The man finally becomes exasperated and decrees that none of the invited guests will be allowed in. He tells his servant, "Go out quickly into the streets and alleys of the town and bring in the poor, the crippled, the blind and the lame" (14:21).

As we have seen, Paul's writings emphasize a very similar point about the power of weakness in Jesus's kingdom. Here we should notice what this story implies about the heavenly banquet. It clearly affirms that impairments will be part of the heavenly celebration. Like Jesus's scars (which we will discuss in the next chapter in more detail), the marks of impairment and being an outsider are not erased in what Jesus explicitly calls the kingdom of God. The outsiders and outcasts are not changed into social elites when they enter the man's banquet. The man welcomes them just as they are, simply because they *want* to be there.

The parable also affirms that it is the impaired and outcast who are actually the first ones, and indeed the only ones, to come and enjoy the banquet. Jesus is inverting ancient (as well as modern) hierarchies of honor, in which people believe that of course a party is better with more eminent guests. The Bible certainly contains affirmations that there will be no more tears in heaven (Rev. 21:4). But why do we assume that having disabilities is something that people *should* cry about? If we've been listening to the many voices of disabled Christians in this book, we will have learned that it is part of their journey to wholeness to have accepted themselves and their bodies. And here we find no hint that wiping tears away means all impairments will be eliminated. Instead, they will be redeemed and made glorious.

Lest this seem a rash statement, consider Mark's rendition of one of Jesus's maxims about the dynamics of salvation. "If your hand causes you to fall into sin, chop it off. It's better for you to enter into life crippled than to go away with two hands into the fire of hell, which can't be put out. If your foot causes you to fall into sin, chop it off. It's better for you to enter life lame than to be thrown into hell with two feet. If your eye causes you to fall into sin, tear it out. It's better for you to enter God's kingdom with one eye than to be thrown into hell with two" (Mark 9:43–47 CEB).

Today plenty of Christians are uncomfortable talking about hell. And almost all would read Jesus's proposal here as a warning about the dire consequences of sin, not as a literal proposal. Yet the tripled repetition by Jesus is a textual sign that this teaching is meant to be taken seriously, perhaps even literally. And through the centuries, many Christians have taken it literally.

Let's put aside for now the distracting questions surrounding hell and Christians actually dismembering themselves. The first hearers of this teaching would not have automatically assumed that being resurrected to an afterlife would mean getting back every body part in a perfect condition.[28] Taken at face value, what seems clear is that Jesus is totally sanguine about people being resurrected with missing body parts. The whole point of the parable is that bodily integrity is worth infinitely less than the integrity of the moral and religious person.

In sum, it seems that in the Bible, physical and even mental "normalcy" is far less interesting than being part of God's rescuing and liberating action in the world. We turn now to look at Christian doctrine to further explore why this might be so.

FOUR

Disability Is a Tragic Effect of the Fall

Disability is a human condition that causes people pain. Not inevitably, but often. People in pain demand a pastoral response from the church. Churches are filled with people who genuinely do want to meet people in pain. This is a wonderful thing. Good Christians respond to people in pain.

Often, however, this pastoral response to disability is not accompanied by a fully thought out theological account of what disability is—or by any theological thought about disability at all. Eventually the lack of theological thought means that even well-meaning pastoral care can take damaging forms. Key aspects of Jesus's healing presence to all kinds of people can be lost. This is how pastoral practices cease to be faithful to Jesus's healing presence to people in need—who may well not desire to be "cured" of their disability.

Over the last few years I've asked a lot of church people to push past their very welcome impulse to be helpful to people with disabilities and to tell me what they think is the most important theological thing to say about disability. After they pause to think, I very often get an answer that goes like this: God created the world good. Adam and Eve sinned. Sin, disease, and death entered the world as a result. Some disabilities arise because the material world now has glitches in it that cause biological mistakes in human development. Other disabilities happen because sinful people do bad things and make mistakes that injure others. In short, disability is one of the many tragic effects of the fall. God didn't want there to be disabilities, but part of God's goodness is to not immediately rectify all this brokenness and sin. God wants to let creatures have their freedom to act and to bear the consequence of their actions.

These are theological claims, and in the abstract they are true. The problem is that this is nearly all the theological thinking most Christians have done about disability. They might have had a few thoughts about "Jesus healing everyone he meets." They have probably heard phrases about heaven being a place where the blind will see and the lame walk.

Given this basic set of theological beliefs, let's take the Christian who holds them and imagine them one more time before a person with disabilities entering a church. In chapter 1 we saw that church people really do believe that they are responsive to people's needs and are often motivated by a strong desire to be genuinely helpful.

But think for a moment about what they are assuming about a disabled person before they have yet exchanged a single word with her or him. Disabled people's lives are a tragic effect of the fall. These tragic effects will be reversed in the resurrection, if not by a miraculous healing anticipating that final resurrection. No wonder the pastoral interventions of good, well-meaning Christians so often miss the mark, given the theological thinness of this starting point!

The standard theological assumptions among Christians about disability is to think the real questions are about the *origins* of disabling conditions. Yet in reality, very, very few people come to church because they want to figure out why there is evil in the world or why they have spent their whole lives in a disabled body. Christians are never going to meet disabled people where they are if they assume that people with a disability are consumed by questions about why they are the way they are. Such questions have no way to offer a theological account of the *goodness* of people's lives *as they are*.

Picture meeting someone with a visible disability in Sunday school or church. If all we have to say about disability concerns brokenness, are we already pitying them? Does this starting point give us anything to say to them? The problem with Christians not thinking theologically about disability is that they end up trapped in wrong—and unanswerable—pastoral questions. Because Christians have often not considered how to think theologically about the goodness of disabled lives as they exist, they don't know how to listen to disabled people or where to focus their pastoral attention. Mayhem ensues.

What Is Theology For?

Few Christians today are sure what a theologian actually does. Pastors often feel threatened by professional theologians. Most Christians can't see how theology actually helps Christians be good Christians. This could be, Ben Conner observes, because many theologians have not really been thinking about the sorts of theologically and pastorally complex questions raised by disability experiences.

> I have come to recognize that the mere presence of a person with a disability on the campus and in the classrooms at a seminary can make people reconsider received biblical interpretations, theological dogma and formulations, and pastoral practices that we had thought were settled and had become ossified in curriculum. Ultimate questions ranging from creation to *telos* ("What does it mean to be made in the image of God?"; "What are the qualifications of a minister?"; "How are disabilities and eschaton related?") must be revisited and reformed in light of the lived experience of disability.[1]

It seems safe to assume that one of the reasons that Christians today find it hard to see what theologians are for is that very few theologians have dared to risk speaking to issues of such direct relevance to contemporary Christians. Disability experiences force theology into territory that is very difficult to live in—and just as hard to explain. The result is that pastoral practice in churches has, with few exceptions, drifted free from the faith it confesses.

The effects of this estrangement of theology and Christian practice are all too evident, as Bethany Fox discovered when she reviewed books about how churches should respond to the disability experience.

> In the collection of how-to books I surveyed about including people with developmental disabilities in church communities, approximately 3 percent of the content in each book covered *why* churches should

include them, and about 97 percent discussed *how* to include them.
There are other books that beautifully make the "why" case . . . but
these tend to remain theoretical without specific, concrete practices
that reflect their theological vision. Most books that do cover concrete
ways to live out this call include a tiny bit of theological rationale,
discussion of biblical passages, or description of the Christian values
that underscore the practice, and then a mountain of information
about logistics, what supplies to buy, how to get volunteers, develop
legal release forms, and a thousand other practical tips.[2]

At one level it makes sense that some books address the theology of
disability while a different set of books addresses the practicalities
of church ministries. It is good that people are searching out either
kind of book, and why should some people not be more interested
in theory while others gravitate toward practice?

This division is problematic for three reasons, suggests Fox. First,
it can only be a work of the Holy Spirit that people want to welcome
people with complex needs into church. Yet that first yearning to
reach out may need to be filled out and solidified by gaining deeper
theological understanding of what such welcome actually entails.
Those Christians hearing the Spirit's call to reach out to people with
disabilities of all sorts deserve to know more about how deeply this
desire is rooted in the heart of Christian faith and Scriptures. Second, without gaining this deeper understanding of the proximity of
disability to the heart of the Christian faith, it is easy for people to
become discouraged, drift on to other projects, or misdirect their ef-
forts. Finally, Christians being drawn by the Spirit into engagement
with the diversity of human life and experience need to be fed from
the riches of Scripture and theology. These riches can lead Christians
into a deeper faithfulness, honing and sharpening our witness.

What is theology for?

> When we forget the connection between what we do and why we do it,
> we can begin to talk about accommodating the needs of people with
> disabilities as an "honorable" act instead of a faithful one. While it
> certainly can be honorable for people to welcome one another, it is
> much more than that. When a practice is merely honorable, it can be
> abandoned when it conflicts with another honorable practice. But

when maintaining a practice is a matter of following the way of Jesus, a community will need imagination and creativity to persist in faithfulness even when complications arise.[3]

Theology serves the church by helping it understand *why* it is doing what it is doing and by giving it the *resources* it needs to *creatively* tackle and *persevere* through the problems it will inevitably face. It is lamentable that theologians have so rarely given themselves to working on the lived experiences of problems of human life. It is especially grievous that this work has barely begun on the theme of disability.

Nancy Eiesland names the task of the theologian with laser-like accuracy: "A theology of disability must be a visible, integral, and ordinary part of the Christian life and our theological reflections on that life. As long as disability is addressed in terms of the themes of sin-disability conflation, virtuous suffering, or charitable action, it will be seen primarily as a fate to be avoided, a tragedy to be explained, or a cause to be championed rather than an ordinary life to be lived."[4] Those are our marching orders. Let's get to it.

The Vulnerability and Weakness of Creatures

When Christians confess that we are creatures, we are affirming a more complex idea than we may suspect. "Nature" is what people who do not believe in God see when they look at the material world. Christians can see that material world too, but we also understand that what we can see is not the same thing as "creation." The distinction is all-important for thinking about disability. Nature makes mistakes, has accidents. But God only creates good things, for the theological reasons outlined in chapter 3.

Amy Jacober learned how important this distinction is through years of discipling disabled teenagers.

> Declaring creation as good is not to bury our heads in the sand and pretend sin does not exist. The converse is also true, declaring that sin exists neither undermines nor negates the fact that creation is good—creation, all creation, every single last one of us is good. And we enter a sinful, fragmented, broken world where God is already present and

about the work of reconciliation. Understanding creation as good is primary in accepting God as good. I have lost count of the number of young adults who have said on hard days that they know God is good but surely *they* somehow were the exception to God's good creation. In other words, they felt like a mistake.[5]

At least one nondisabled theologian seems to have arrived at this insight rather earlier than the rest of us: Dietrich Bonhoeffer. It is by now well known that in September of 1939 Hitler promulgated his infamous euthanasia decree, code-named "T4." Bonhoeffer had long seen it coming. Five years before, he had preached to his London congregation, "What is the meaning of weakness in this world, what is the meaning of physical or mental or moral weakness? . . . Have we ever realized that ultimately our whole attitude toward life, toward man and God depends on the answer to this problem?"[6] Bonhoeffer was attuned to the issue of disability because he had a genuine conversion experience during a stay for a theological gathering that had been held at a large Christian home specializing in the care of epileptics, the Bethel Sanitorium.

He described an experience worshiping in this community that "made a deep impression" on him in a letter he wrote home to his grandmother in 1933. When the community gathers for worship, he tells her, there are large numbers of people with epilepsy and other mental illnesses, as well as the nurses and carers who are sprinkled through the very large crowd.

> Here we have a part of the church that still knows what the church can be about and what it cannot be about. . . . It is an extraordinary sight, the nurses who are there to help in case one of them falls; then there are elderly tramps who come in off the country roads, the theological students, the children from the lab school, doctors and pastors with their families. But the sick people dominate the picture, and they are keen listeners and participants. Their experience of life must be most extraordinary, not having control over their bodies, having to be resigned to the possibility of an attack at any moment. Today in church was the first time this really struck me, as I became aware of these moments. Their situation of being truly defenseless perhaps gives these people a much clearer insight into certain realities of human existence, the fact

that we are indeed basically defenseless, than can be possible for healthy persons. And it is just this abrupt alternation between standing there healthy and falling down sick, which must be more conducive to this insight than being healthy all the time. There is nothing sentimental about any of this; it is tremendously real and natural. It knocks down some of the barriers with which we usually shut ourselves off from this world. Here it simply is a part of one's own life, as it is in reality.[7]

Worshiping with people with intellectual disabilities revealed once and for all to Bonhoeffer the demonic aspirations of the National Socialist regime. German Christians now faced a basic conflict between being a German nationalist or being a Christian. The most dangerous outcome would be to conceal the intrinsic conflict between the Christian view of disabled life and the increasingly powerful desire to make Germany great again.

When it came, Bonhoeffer recognized Aktion T4 as a governmental declaration of war against institutions that cared for people with disabilities. It literally paved a road toward their alternative: the extermination camps.

Bonhoeffer's experience in Christian worship alongside people with disabilities had given a man who had grown up among the elite a view from the bedside. He had climbed up on the chariot with the Ethiopian eunuch. And because he had, he could see with crystal clarity how political rhetoric and bureaucratic processes were being used to destroy the weakest. It was an experience that was to solidify disability as a focal point of Bonhoeffer's theology. Vulnerability had to be taken seriously if the Christian gospel was to make real-world sense.

Bonhoeffer discovered two claims that remain important for any theology of disability. First, the church is not an ideal community but a community made up of a wide array of people. It does not seek to be homogenous. Instead, it must continually learn what it means to remain together in loving communion despite sometimes quite radical differences. This is Bonhoeffer's ecclesiological realism. Second, Bonhoeffer saw that the only way to talk about what it means to be human (anthropology) was through Christology. Only the true man, the head of the one body of the church, can show us what it means to be a body in diversity.[8]

The Lament of Vulnerable Creatures

To be a creature is to be limited, needy, woundable, and susceptible to illness. *Vulnerability* is thus an anthropological constant. It is a universal characteristic of the creaturely state. *Woundedness* is the enacted state of reduction to which vulnerability exposes creatures.

One important implication of the state of sin is the powerful desire that rises up in human beings to become "like God"—to surmount our woundable condition. The other, more faithful response to being woundable is to lament. To affirm a Christian confession of creation teaches us that we ought not lament the *person* or *existence* that any one of us has been given. Yet as woundable creatures we very well may feel the strong need to lament the *road* that we or those we love must travel, as emphasized by Tim Wright, father of a son with profound physical and intellectual disabilities.

> In the next couple of months, Sam will be having two major operations on his hips. It will be a time of long stays in hospital. We will be split between our children at home and Sam in hospital over an hour away. If all goes to plan, Sam will be in hospital for seven to ten days for each operation, one week apart. He will endure both of his legs being broken and then pinned in place, and possibly a bone graft. He won't be able to lie on his side like he has for the last decade; instead he will be placed in traction and suffer pain he is unable to fully express. We know it is coming, yet we can't explain it to him.
>
> "Oh, bother, that's less than ideal" simply doesn't cut it.
>
> When our friends ask me how I feel about this, it's much more likely I will give an honest and heartfelt stream of swearwords. . . .
>
> It is good to lament, to cry out to God in anguish, but too often we want to skip the hard emotions and focus on the brighter ones. Sometimes we are even fooled into thinking this is what God wants us to do too. But instead of our Sunday best, God longs for us to come before Him dressed in the full robes of authenticity and honesty.[9]

Lament is a recognition that what is *hard* for creatures is not necessarily *bad* for them, continues Sam's mother, Rachel. "Transformation, sacrifice and refining all seem to require the hard road, because that is where the hope and perseverance is tended and grown. It's the rough roads that bring the best view, not the easy one. Quite simply, if we want the power of the resurrection, we have to walk through the transformation of the cross."[10] The vulnerability of creatures that makes them liable to be wounded is the place of transformation. How we respond to threats to our vulnerability is one of the places where our faith has to grow. One of the dynamics of sin is its power to wrap us up in nursing and protecting our wounds. This can lead to anger, depression, aggression, or withdrawal. It is in community that our woundedness is healed. This healing, however, is only accessible to those who repentantly acknowledge that we are both vulnerable (by nature) and wounded (have been actually harmed in some way)—that is, we must admit that we are sinners, not in principle but in fact.

In *Jesus*, God became vulnerable by becoming flesh. This taking on of "woundability" was the condition for his being "wounded for our transgressions" (Isa. 53:5 KJV). Jesus also revealed the difference between vulnerability and sin because "when he was reviled, [he] reviled not" (1 Pet. 2:23 KJV). In this, Jesus makes visible the central theological core of healing communities.

Because Jesus is the eternal God, he cannot be entirely swallowed by creaturely vulnerability. The eternal God persists and promises to restore human beings to their true creaturehood. Hannah Goodliff observes,

> Our culture celebrates being strong, independent and successful in all areas of life, but more and more I've come to realise that we were not built to live this way. Vulnerability and brokenness are inevitable. When we accept our own weaknesses, and allow others to draw alongside us, the result can be something truly beautiful.
>
> There is a danger in trying to present ourselves as a perfect, finished article—we protect others from seeing our vulnerabilities and fail to love each other in the truest sense. We don't have to pretend that we can do life alone. God gave us the Church—a bunch of broken people who, together, are being transformed by "the grace of the Lord Jesus Christ, and the love of God, and the fellowship of the Holy Spirit" (2 Cor. 13:14). It's messy, it's unpredictable and it doesn't always follow the script but it's beautiful, and gradually I am learning to become better at asking for and accepting help.[11]

To confess that we are creatures is to confess that to exist is good, no matter what form our bodies or minds take. This does not mean that we will not be wounded. We will be tempted to set up defensive walls to hide the pain of wounds already sustained and to protect ourselves from receiving new ones. To do so, however, is a sinful self-isolation that ultimately cuts us off from ourselves and others.

In lament we can instead remain open to God by expressing our suffering and pain. In keeping the lines of communication open with God, we are prepared to also expose our hurts to the community of God's people. We will soon dwell at more length on how God's people can offer deep healing, even if there is no cure for what ails us.

Disability and Sin

Before leaving the topic of sin, it is important to directly face the problem with which this chapter opened. For many Christians, sin is the first doctrine that comes to mind when the topic of disability comes up. Now that we have surveyed the biblical themes related to disability, we can see that to focus on sin as the main doctrine for describing disability is not only biblically wrong but pastorally disastrous. But sin is part of the equation.

We can understand the place of sin and disability only if we have robustly affirmed, first, that God loves everyone who exists as they are, even in a fallen world. Second, nobody's life can be understood if we only talk about sin. Sin impacts every human life equally. It is grossly unfair to think that some people's lives are more comprehensively explained by talking about the effects of sin than others.

Christians do confess the fallenness of human beings and so are right to think that it has *something* to do with disability. The question is how. The biblical witness affirms that being a creature means limit, birth and death, growth and decay, and illness and accident. The fall accounts in Genesis 3–4 that stretch all the way to the idolatrous fall into linguistic division at Babel in Genesis 11 make one thing abundantly clear: affirming sin as an elaborated feature of broken human relations leads Christians to expect that sin will leave painful marks on other people's bodies. That the cascading effects of sin all end up marking human bodies is highlighted early in the fall accounts in the brutal image of Cain battering his brother Abel to death (Gen. 4:2–16).

When Christians confess the world to be fallen, one thing we are confessing is that we can break and maim others' bodies. That is the origin of some disabilities. Human beings may also be born with effects that spring from the brokenness of the material realm. This is tricky territory and easy to get badly wrong. If we talk about the sinful brokenness of creation in a way that negates the goodness of existence altogether, then we will fall off one side into Manichean dualism. That is the traditional name for the idea that God is not all powerful and that there are other powers whom he cannot defeat— evil powers. The claim that some people's very existence is corrupted amounts to saying that God could not stop another evil god from creating corrupted beings.

There is a more practical danger when Christians lose the affirmation that to exist is good: they are no longer able to resist the cultural drive that disability activists call "kill or cure." The starting assumption of the "kill or cure" mindset is that some lives are nothing more than one long suffering due to the condition of their bodies and minds. If we can't cure them—so eradicating the intrinsic evil of suffering by curing a disabling condition—then it is best that they not exist. We can eradicate their suffering by not allowing them to be born or by allowing them to kill themselves through practices like euthanasia.

There is another way that an account of sin can veer off the other side of the road. This is called the Pelagian misreading of the fall. Pelagians deny the severity of the fall. They believe the world is not so broken that we cannot fix it.

The medical perspective on disability often steers people toward a Pelagian position. In modern medicine, bodies are meant to work within a range of normal parameters, and there is no reason why we can't reset and reshape every body to get it working as it should. Where there is the will and the technique, we can fix everything—even death. In the medical model, sin is located in malformed materiality. Through its powerful techniques, medicine can get broken and malformed materiality running normally again.

The social model of disability, which has arisen to combat the dominance of the medical model, denies the presumption at the root of the medical model—that there is one sort of "normal" body. There are all sorts of bodies, the defenders of this model say. What disables is the ways human beings treat each other. If we can reshape our societies so that no one is excluded, then we will have eradicated disability, because bodily and mental difference are really not a problem. In the social model of disability, sin is solely located in the injustice and ostracization of some in society. Sin is the injustice of the majority who make it impossible for people with some kinds of bodies to participate in society.

The Manichean response to disability is to call it a failure, an evil, and to try to get rid of it. The Pelagian response to disability is to say that everything can and will be fixed. A Christian account of creation, sin, and disability insists that things are more complicated.

God makes us with limits and gives us form, which God decrees good. Because bodies come in a range of forms, each has its own challenges and pains. The confession of sin also means that bodies can be damaged in ways that cannot be fixed. To be sinful creatures means that we should expect our bodies to, sooner or later, not always do what we want them to do.

The crucial thing to keep in mind is that getting sin and disability right is primarily a matter of never undermining the "it was good" of God's decree over what God has created. Getting sin and disability right thus entails resisting being drawn into the wrong questions. The question of disability and sin is not answered by asking, "Where did disability come from?" It is not answered by any direct linkage of disability with sin. We understand sin and disability rightly by constantly asking, "What is a kingdom reaction to sin? How can we enact the image of Christ's response to sin?" In other words, we don't understand sin until we understand the redemption and healing offered in Jesus Christ.

Imaging God

Most Christians think first of the doctrine of sin when asked about disability, since it seems to explain the existence of disability. The second doctrine that usually springs to mind is the image of God. The image of God seems the perfect theological idea with which to affirm the value and intrinsic worth of every human being.

And this is indeed what the first chapter of the Bible seems to say, when God says on the sixth day of creation,

> "Let us make [humankind] in our image, in our likeness, so that they may rule over the fish in the sea and the birds in the sky, over the livestock and all the wild animals, and over all the creatures that move along the ground."

> So God created [humankind] in his own image,
>   in the image of God he created them;
>   male and female he created them. (Gen. 1:26–27)

But what exactly is the image that appears here to be granted to every human being? This is where Christians trying to explain disability have gotten into trouble.

There are three main ways that the image of God has been defined over the centuries of Christianity. The first has been called the substantive view. In this view human beings have many capacities, but God has distinguished human beings from all other sorts of creatures by giving them capacities that no other creatures have. Theologians have argued over what that capacity is. Some have argued that rationality is the capacity that distinguishes humans from all other creatures, others the human sense for morality, the capacity for religious sense or worship, and even the upright physical posture. The capacity to reason has been the most regular nominee for the trait that most obviously signals the presence of the divine image in human beings.

In recent decades the substantive view has been challenged "from below," in that scientific observation has allowed us to learn that one or another animal has almost every human trait you can think of. More problematically, if we are committed to a definition of the image of God as localized in those capacities of humans that other animals do not have, then only the highest performing humans can be said to have it. The substantive view of the image of God seems to commit Christian theology to a best-case scenario in which only the best and the brightest human beings can be said to exhibit the image of God clearly.

In other words, this view creates all sorts of problems when trying to think clearly about disability. Whichever specific trait or capacity that marks human beings as having the image of God will leave out someone with some disability. This account seems to demand that we say that they are not worthy of the same respect and value as others.

The functionalist view of the image of God keys off another feature in Genesis 1: the fact that God gives human beings a task. The language of the image of God is not assumed to be an intrinsic possession of every human being but points to a royal calling. To image God is something that must be undertaken through "ruling over the fish in the sea and the birds in the sky, over the livestock and all the wild animals, and over all the creatures that move along the ground" (1:26).

This definition of the image of God, however, comes perilously close to disenfranchising those who are not-able-to-do. There are certainly some human beings whose mental or physical state makes it hard if not impossible to do anything that might be called "having dominion"—which most defenders of this position understand to be something like shaping culture.

A third view tries to take the problems of the substantive and functional views into account by focusing on a different aspect of the passage, specifically Genesis 1:27. Those holding a relational view of the image of God highlight the phrase where God deliberates about making the human species in God's "image." After this phrase comes "male and female he created them." In this view human beings are made for relationship, with each other and with God. It is through life-giving relationships across difference that human beings image Christ to one another.

This view affirms all human creatures as special in having been the only creatures given the task of imaging God in the world. The birth of every human being from Adam and Eve marks their bodies as human, and human beings have a task: not to subdue the earth, necessarily, but to live in Christlike ways toward one another. This relational view is an attempt to acknowledge the reality that the New Testament never assumes that human beings securely possess the image of God. Instead, human beings are called to conform to *Christ's* image, as Paul explains.

> The god of this age has blinded the minds of unbelievers, so that they cannot see the light of the gospel that displays the glory of Christ,

who is the image of God. For what we preach is not ourselves, but
Jesus Christ as Lord, and ourselves as your servants for Jesus' sake.
For God, who said, "Let light shine out of darkness," made his light
shine in our hearts to give us the light of the knowledge of God's
glory displayed in the face of Christ. But we have this treasure in jars
of clay to show that this all-surpassing power is from God and not
from us. (2 Cor. 4:4–7)

The New Testament in fact uses the language of the image of God
far more often than the Old Testament and always presents it as something to which every human is called. Notice how far the biblical use
of the term "image of God" goes beyond the language of "human
rights" or "universal human worth." Humans are valuable not because
they have God's image but because God made them in order that they
should display Christ's love in the world.

A biblically informed account of the image of God does highlight
who humans were created to be but only in order to emphasize the
importance of sanctification. If we desire to "include" everyone in
our definition of humanity, this cannot be done by constructing a
universal ethical code or by expelling those who do not seem to fit
the image we have of "normal" humans. Only by being visited by
the one true man on the cross is the image restored to those who no
longer know how to display the way of being in the world that he
displayed—despite this having been the very thing for which every
human has been created. The human being is defined not by their
attributes, their dispositions, or their capabilities but by the image
that God has promised to *bestow on them in Christ*. Disability experiences have helped contemporary theologians do justice to the
richness of the biblical tradition in affirming that bodily difference
and uniqueness are part of each person's vocation. The idea of the
image of God is therefore a reminder that God loves difference and
calls *every* human being to be conformed to Christ.

If Christians today want to get the image of God and disability
right, they must banish the question, "Does this person have the capacity to image God?" People with all sorts of disabilities, including
learning difficulties, may powerfully image Christ. The New Testament's call to "put on" Christ (Gal. 3:27 KJV) aims at the *restoration*

of the image of God in us. "Image of God" language is not a statement of a given but a call to responsibility, a call into a loving quality of relationship. Christians today get the image of God and disability right when they ask, "Does the way I look at people bring the gaze of Christ into the world? Does the way I speak to people let Christ's voice be heard? Does the way I touch people build them up?"

Imaging and the Least Presentable Members

Plenty of people will be scratching their heads about what it actually means to say, "Does the way I look at people bring the gaze of Christ into the world?" The remarkable fact, however, is that this language seems to pop up wherever Christians find themselves drawn into communion with people with disabilities.

As a young Chinese Christian, Xin Wei felt herself being called to support an orphanage housing several disabled children in Hebei province. She soon had a growing sense that the Lord was asking her to do more. In August 2009, Xin Wei and her husband, Steve, used their savings and the funds of friends from all walks of life to start a home exclusively for children with disabilities outside the town of Da Dian in Shandong province. They called it Home of Mephibosheth.

As Xin Wei explains in the award-winning movie about the home, children with complex needs are often abandoned in China.[12] If they happen to be rescued, they are often cared for in the most squalid and insufficient group homes imaginable. In China, providing top-quality care to disabled children is by no means common sense. Some children are just too hard, too much of a burden.

In setting up the Home of Mephibosheth, Xin Wei and Steve were thus witness to a noticeably distinct way of life. At the root of this way of life is an understanding of the image of God very like the one I have just set out. In Xin Wei's words,

> Many people come here and look around. They often say, "How pitiable the children are!" "How admirable you are!" I say, "Here, there are no pitiable children, and there are no admirable people. There is only One who is admirable, and He is God. We are merely people covered by his grace, because our love, patience and hope are from

Him." When we look at these children through the eyes of Jesus, we discover that we need them far more than they need us. On the surface it looks as if we are serving the children. In reality we are serving Jesus Himself. Jesus is hidden within the lives of these children, and He is watching us.[13]

The Gospel of John provides a similarly concrete picture of the ways of Jesus in this world. John offers imagery that guides Christians into the essential heart of the life that displays—images—Christ in this world. Jesus's ministry is coming to its climactic moment. He must now undergo his passion on the cross. His time teaching his disciples in the flesh is at an end. In his last moment with them, he does something they will remember, something that encapsulates who he is. He shows them what he wants from them as he returns to the Father.

In this act we see all the threads pulled together that I have emphasized in my reading of disability in the Bible. Here we see Jesus himself showing the form of human relationships that make his image present in the world. Jesus washes his disciples' feet: "Jesus knew that the Father had put all things under his power, and that he had come from God and was returning to God; so he got up from the meal, took off his outer clothing, and wrapped a towel around his waist. After that, he poured water into a basin and began to wash his disciples' feet, drying them with the towel that was wrapped around him" (John 13:3–5).

The two parts of this passage seem not to connect—"[knowing] that the Father had put all things under his power . . . [he] began to wash his disciples' feet" (John 13:3, 5). Why does washing feet have anything to do with Jesus having the power of God? The writer of the Gospel of John wants us to see that the heart of the highest and most transcendent essence of God plays out in worldly, mundane acts. Jesus will go to the cross, but his will be the final sacrifice. All those who will follow him will do so by participating in his very mundane loving in the world.

Jesus's mundane act of washing feet is once again a nonverbal act. His love and commitment to the disciples is *done*, not *said*. We recall his taking others by the hand as he heals them. This is touch that heals and upbuilds through acts of service. Even the most learning impaired can feel the love in the hands of the one who bathes them.

Jesus does not offer them a full bath or, like we do, just wash their hands before they eat. He zeros in on their feet. This is important to get if we want to image Christ in relation to disability. In the ancient world, the feet were one of the unsightly members, usually dirty from walking on unpaved surfaces. That's the logic behind Paul saying, "The head cannot say to the feet, 'I don't need you!' On the contrary, those parts of the body that seem to be weaker are indispensable, and the parts that we think are less honorable we treat with special honor. And the parts that are unpresentable are treated with special modesty, while our presentable parts need no special treatment" (1 Cor. 12:21–24).

This passage makes little sense to us today, because we think of feet in a more morally neutral way, as just another body part. But Paul's labeling of the feet as the less honorable or the unpresentable member reveals that in the ancient world feet shared with the genitals an unenviable reputation.

The assumption at the time that the feet were less honorable also explains the shocking nature of the vignette that John presents as a warm-up act for Jesus's washing of the disciples' feet. "Then Mary took about a pint of pure nard, an expensive perfume; she poured it on Jesus' feet and wiped his feet with her hair. And the house was filled with the fragrance of the perfume" (John 12:3). The act is shocking because touching someone's less honorable members is necessarily a vulnerable and intimate act. Mary's nonverbal act displays in potent terms her devotion and worship. Mary has focused her attention on the lowest part of Jesus, not daring to presume upon him. The love in her touch is clear from her using her own hair to dry his feet. It is such a luminous act that it fills the house with its fragrance.

Returning to Jesus's last supper with his disciples, we find a protest breaking out. Peter first resists the Son of God washing his feet. When Jesus replies that if he does not, Peter will "have no part with me" (John 13:8), Peter offers what can only be called a comedic comeback: "Then, Lord, . . . not just my feet but my hands and my head as well!" (13:9).

Peter has managed to thoroughly misunderstand what is going on. First, he thinks it is degrading for his teacher and religious superior to wash his least presentable body parts. Then, when his own interest is at stake, he goes entirely the other way and wants as much as he can get. His dual misunderstanding makes it important to listen to Jesus's reply, which establishes a very different hierarchy of values than those that motivate Peter. "Jesus answered, 'Those who have had a bath need only wash their feet'" (John 13:10).

To those of us in the modern world, this is a nonsense answer. A bath or a shower is for the whole body; anything less is not a bath. No doubt ancient readers also knew that having a full-body bath is not the same thing as having a body part washed.

Jesus is making a theological point. If the least presentable members have been honored, the whole body is clean. Jesus is not leaving his disciples with a hygiene lesson, redefining what counts as a bath. He is engaged in a symbolic act. He is showing them something essential about how the members of the body of Christ must relate to one another. Read in this way we can see what a potent point he is making about how the church is to relate to the "least honored" among us. If those who are assumed to be least valuable are taken care of and honored, then the whole body is right with God.

We must be careful not to slip back into the charity model of disability, in which disabled people are again set apart as full-time recipients of the charity of the church. That is not what Jesus is saying.

We know that the church is living as the body of Christ when its least presentable members occupy a place of honor. That is what makes the whole church pleasing in the sight of God. "Washing," then, is standing in here for all acts of service that upbuild another member of the body of Christ. The sequence is important here. First, we have been redeemed by God's act of serving us. "Unless I wash you, you have no part with me" (John 13:8). In being washed, we are then made servants of God's love for others. "Now that I, your Lord and Teacher, have washed your feet, you also should wash one another's feet. I have set you an example that you should do as I have done for you" (13:14–15).

It would be tempting to read this passage as an invitation merely to imitate Jesus's acts, as if imaging God were a matter of doing the things that the first-century Jew named Jesus did. John heads that reading off directly in the next chapter.

In enacting service that upbuilds others, Christians are partaking of God's ongoing, redemptive work in Jesus through the Spirit. "Anyone who does not love me will not obey my teaching. . . . All this I have spoken while still with you. But the Advocate, the Holy Spirit, whom the Father will send in my name, will teach you all things and will remind you of everything I have said to you" (John 14:24–26).

Put simply: imaging God means becoming people who see each person as Christ sees them, who act toward them with the outreaching love that Christ has for them. As Peter puts it, "Each of you has received a gift to use to serve others. Be good servants of God's various gifts of grace. Anyone who speaks should speak words from God. Anyone who serves should serve with the strength God gives so that in everything God will be praised through Jesus Christ. Power and glory belong to him forever and ever. Amen" (1 Pet. 4:10–11 NCV).

The writer of John places the story of Jesus washing the disciples' feet at the hinge of his Gospel for a reason. He wants to hammer home the point that the culmination of what Jesus teaches his disciples is a matter of slowing down to care for the state of the least presentable members. This is what it means to partake of Christ: to be seeking out, one relationship at a time, a community in which the least presentable parts know themselves loved—and so feel free to give what they have to the body in return.

In chapter 5 we will dive deeper into the practicalities of being a community of hope. Jesus's loving care for the least presentable members is a practical gesture that invites hope in the whole body.

The poet Paul Murray observes that though we may think that we know what despair and hope are, Jesus's example asks us to consider the depth of Christian hope that is enacted when people tenderly get down on their knees to wash the feet and dress the wounds of those "who will not walk tomorrow."[14] In a society that constantly urges us to move on, Murray urges us to sit with the hope that is on display when someone attends to those who will not be able to perform, to move on, to make an impression. To give care and attention to those we have accepted might never be physically healed at least calls forth a giving up of our own agendas. That surrender evokes deep tenderness. It is an offer of communion. In its ripeness it is a life-giving exchange between us and God.

That we so often resist this engagement makes it critical for non-disabled Christians to reflect on Peter's initial resistance to being washed by Jesus. Instinctively, Peter recoils from handing over his less-presentable parts to Jesus's ministrations. Those of us who think of ourselves as "able" are seldom ready to let God, or others, see those parts that embarrass us.

Peter reveals the hidden symmetry between how comfortable we sinners are assuming that we are the ones who are functional and capable—as we define "functional"—and the impulse to hide our vulnerabilities from God. Peter's reaction to Jesus's request shows Christians how our sense that our own inabilities and embarrassing vulnerabilities should be hidden and protected is precisely what keeps us from perceiving the subtlety and breadth of the love of Christ that is foolishness to the world.

We will shortly return to dwell again on Peter's hint that we cannot give up the sinful illusion that we are capable and "able" without being confronted by the gifts of the Spirit.

Can Disabled People Have Faith?

Many Christians imagine having faith as a matter of believing something to be true. Christianity certainly assumes a set of truth claims about the world. The definition of being an unbeliever is to not believe these truths.

The problem comes when we think about people who appear unable to understand anything as complex as the Christian creed. Some seem not to have the capacity to do the simple thing that Paul says in Romans 10:9 is the basic act of Christian faith: "If you declare with your mouth, 'Jesus is Lord,' and believe in your heart that God raised him from the dead, you will be saved."

There is a tradition within Christianity of meeting this problem by saying that those who are not capable of praying such a prayer are also not capable of sinning. This is the "holy innocents" tradition. The holy innocents tradition tends to romanticize the ones it calls "innocent" as angels who are incapable of doing wrong. Its dark side is the tendency to see the same people as animals incapable of redemption should they not act so innocently as people believe they should.

What this holy innocents tradition shares with the modern medicalized accounts of disability discussed in chapter 2 is a focusing of the question of health and salvation on the individual. Faith is defined as the capacity to perform a set of crucial acts, whether in the heart, in the mind, or in church.

Another way to approach those who seem to not have the capacity to confess the name of Jesus is to emphasize that human beings were created to image Christ, and Christ is a body, a grouping. "The more emphasis that is placed on belief, particularly for individuals, the more learning-impaired people are marginalized," Stanley Hauerwas has observed. Yet Christians might also say that

> learning-impaired people challenge the church to remember . . . that what saves is not our personal existential commitments, but being a member of a body constituted by practices more determinative than my "personal" commitment.
>
> I suspect this is the reason why learning-impaired people often are better-received in more "liturgical" traditions—that is, traditions which know that what God is doing through the community's ritual is more determinative than what any worshiper brings to or receives from the ritual. After all, the God worshiped is the Spirit that cannot be subject to human control. The liturgy of the church is ordered to be open to such wildness by its hospitality to that Spirit. What learning-impaired people might do to intrude onto that order is nothing compared to what the Spirit has done and will continue to do.[15]

The next section will develop in more detail what is implied in Hauerwas's crucial reminder that we can expect the Spirit to disrupt the "normal" way of things, including in the church. We will see that this is an extremely promising disruption.

Hauerwas's main point, however, is to highlight the importance of repeated rituals in helping many people with special needs find their place in church. Routine is a gift to the church, and many people with disabilities (autism, for example) need strict routine, which is a reminder of the gift of repeated liturgies.

Amy Jacober highlights how this works, relating one story from her work as a summer camp counselor.

> One particular high school girl came to camp just days after her house had burned down and she and her family had to be rescued from it. It also happened to be that she has autism. She had several difficult moments throughout the week for a variety of reasons. Yet, when it came time for evening service, she settled. She was not crying or worried about the fire, what would happen when she went home, or what was going on around her. In fact, she was able to help others know what to do or what was coming as she knew the rhythm and ritual of the evening service so well. I was hanging out with her cabin and asked her once how she knew all of the prayers and what to do and say. She giggled a little and said, "I just know it! I do it because I know it and I know because I do it." I wondered as well if she was simply offering rote memory or if there was meaning attached, so I asked. She then went on to explain every element of the service in ways that were simple but not simplistic. She had been shaped and was shaping the other girls in her cabin not by studying and persuading, but by living the very rhythms she had caught over years of being shaped.[16]

The crucial point to notice is that the assent of faith and, indeed, genuine theological understanding *can* emerge for the individual through immersion in the life of the worshiping community.

It can also be true that if we pay attention, we will discover individuals affirming their faith in unexpected ways. The girl in Jacober's account knows the liturgy. Others may go forward for communion. What Christians must learn to do is to see that God came to humans in the flesh of Jesus Christ. Human beings, every human being, can receive and welcome Christ in the flesh. And every human being can, in Christ, welcome others.

This is why, if we affirm that everyone is created to image God, we must also affirm that every human being is capable of following the Lordship of Jesus by embracing their place in the body of Christ.

Often nonliturgical or low-church traditions include practices that are simply assumed to be inaccessible to those with learning impairments, such as discipleship practices. Yet as Jacober observes, to deprive those with disabilities of access to such basic activities of Christian discipleship is a failure of imagination.

> Discipleship alongside those with disabilities can be a creative, freeing experience. One of my very favorite examples of this comes from a friend who refused to see limitations for the girls in her group. Suzanne Williams is the Regional Young Life Capernaum Director in the Nashville area. In addition to her regular duties leading Club, a youth group experience for people with disabilities, she led a discipleship group. The girls in her group each had their own unique personalities, likes and dislikes, just like other adolescents. What they each also had was a disability of some sort. Suzanne refused that to be what defined them or their ability to align their lives around God. She invited each girl to choose a project in their discipleship group that had to meet at least one of three categories. It must: 1) glorify God; 2) grow their faith; or 3) serve others. The young women took this very seriously, studying and talking about what this meant for a year. They prayed for one another as each girl chose a project. This was not a one-off service afternoon. It was an intense time of community where not only the lives of the young women were changed, but so many around them.[17]

Many low-church traditions have a regular practice of giving testimony. If we allow that people with intellectual difficulties and other sorts of disabilities can develop in their faith, then there is no reason to exclude them from giving testimony, Jacober observes.

> Testimony creates a space for authentic storytelling and for the community to affirm and correct those portions that relate to God. Testimony also invites the community to do some self-reflection and consider where their stories warrant affirmation or correction. The cost in testimony is that not everyone will truly listen. To listen requires active presence and the ability to hear someone's story on its own terms. It demands that we not overlay our presuppositions and experiences on someone else. It invites us into the diverse world created by God. This can feel too risky for some. Risky or not, it is what is required. Testimony should give a safe space for those with disabilities to find and practice their voice so they may use it in the world outside of the church. This, too, is a spiritual act of service. This, too, is the act of a disciple.[18]

Allowing people with disabilities to give testimony is also a stark reminder that the Spirit raises up people to speak of God. Letting people give testimony may lead them to discover their vocation to preach the gospel.

Lorraine Williams is the pastor of a Deaf congregation within a Los Angeles Pentecostal megachurch. She had been called to serve Deaf people, believing that they deserved to be fully part of the church. For many years she threw herself into signing in services, and over the years a substantial number of Deaf people had been attracted to the church. One year Lorraine decided the time was ripe to take her Deaf congregants on a mission trip. They decided on Jamaica, which was perfect because the people there spoke American Sign Language and there were precious few interpreters in churches. After months of fundraisers, the time finally came to board the plane. They would be sharing their stories and the gospel with people who had never had Jesus explained in their own language—sign language.

Many of these Deaf Christians had never told their stories before. They had worshiped alongside thousands of hearing congregants at their church in California who had never thought to ask them to share their stories, their testimonies, their struggles. Their pastor had even said on a radio show that no Deaf person would preach in his pulpit.

Sadly, such sentiments from pastors are not as marginal as we might hope. Blind people often hear the same objections to their ministry, observes John Hull. Research has shown that ordination selection panels in the Church of England have in recent memory held the view that "a priest or minister is meant to care for others, but a blind person needs caring for. How can you care for others when you yourself need care?"[19]

It is important to recognize how socially marginalizing being Deaf often is. Hearing people often think Deaf people sound odd when they talk, and sometimes assume they are learning impaired. What is abundantly clear is that it takes time for a hearing person to understand what a Deaf person is trying to say, and it is a rare hearing Christian who will slow down enough to become friends with a Deaf person.

So for an overwhelmingly hearing congregation with a famous preacher and a world-class choir and band—why would they want to hear Deaf people preach? These are the reasons why these Deaf Christians had to go all the way to Jamaica to find a church where they could tell their testimonies of being claimed as followers of Christ.

As they did so, something happened that they did not expect. As Christians who had lived on the margins of their own church life shared their testimonies, they discovered for the first time that they were not just recipients. They were more than recipients of the care of a "special ministry" financially supported by the "normal" church. Because they had a word of Jesus to share, they were not just riding on the coattails of a much larger, louder, and more flashy group of participants in the worship service.

Their journeys with God could build up others. Their stories of redemption from the loneliness and abuse that so often besets Deaf minorities powerfully affected others. They even had something to say that the rest of the congregation needed to hear—whether they wanted to or not!

Thus, it was through the process of sharing their testimonies that these Deaf Christians had their assumptions overturned about who the "real" church is. They discovered the falsity of their previous assumption that they were in church because of the generosity and forbearance of the "real" church that had included them. The truth was that they had something that their home church wasn't aware it needed.

Some even realized that they might be called to be ministers. Being invited to speak publicly of their walk with God had shattered their sense that they needed to be "included." They already belonged, and they had a word from God that the body of Christ needed.

Perhaps God will have mercy on a Western church facing shrinking numbers of ordinands if it learns to discern the Spirit's call on lives that have for too long been seen as not capable of being ministers of the gospel. Or maybe, as the Jesuit priest Michael Buckley put in a 1971 talk to seminarians, the church needs to ask, "Is this man weak enough to be a priest?"[20] It is a question that goes to the heart of what we think it means to be a minister of the gospel of Jesus Christ. "For we do not have a high priest who is unable to empathize with our weaknesses, but we have one who has been tempted in every way, just as we are, yet he did not sin. . . . He is able to deal gently with those who are ignorant and are going astray, since he himself is [beset with] weakness" (Heb. 4:15; 5:2; see also 2:18).

Spiritual Gifts as the Essence of Church

Some readers may have gotten the impression by this point in the chapter that being redeemed and made to image Christ can be understood in individual terms. That *I* need to become someone who images Christ in the world. In fact, as Jesus's own teaching and practice conveys, being a Christian is not an individual affair but a collective one. We are to be a community imaging Christ by washing one another's feet—by serving one another, especially those who are outsiders in our society.

The apostle Paul's account of the role of the gifts of the Spirit is the bridge that we need to get from Jesus's teaching that we are to wash one another's feet to a rounded picture of what the interpersonal order of human life looks like when it is incorporated into Christ.

What kind of community emerges when we are all imaging Christ to one another? Paul's central concern in 1 Corinthians 12 is to answer this question. To appreciate this chapter, we have to be wary of the many ways modern individualism leads us to misread the Bible. In the case of this chapter, the dangerous assumption is the one many Christians instinctively make—assuming that when the Bible speaks about spiritual gifts, it is talking about obvious sorts of skills recognized by everyone.

We say, "She's a gifted athlete," or "He has the gift of teaching." What we mean is that some people have skills to get things done well and that these skills are widely recognized in society. This picture focuses attention on individuals and what capacities they have or don't have.

This is not a Christian account of the gifts of the Spirit. Our first hint that it is not biblical is noticing how inevitably it positions those with disabilities as somehow needing to be "included" despite their having few, if any, gifts. This theology plays right into the problems we have already seen that attend disability language, with its tendency to solidify hierarchies of ability.

The fatal theological mistake is the conflation of what society considers a gift with the gifts of the Holy Spirit. This is a misunderstanding not only of the gifts of the Spirit but also of what it means to be the body of Christ. This misunderstanding of the gospel is at the heart of Christians' inability to appreciate disabled people.

Saint Paul offers a very different picture of spiritual gifts. Paul wrote 1 Corinthians to a church in Corinth that was, in important respects, much like the modern church. The Corinthian church was divided among groups that each wanted to make one or the other natural skill the premiere spiritual gift. One group wanted those who were good at lofty speaking to be recognized as the "really" spiritual ones, while another group wanted those who could get the crowd worked up into an emotional fever pitch to be held up as the paradigmatic Christians. This fight over which skill would be considered the "most spiritual" was causing plenty of bickering.

Christians today don't tend to think of it in these terms. In our more honest moments, however, we can admit to comparing ourselves to other people on the basis of our education, our successes at work, or even our appearance and the car we drive. If we assume that these markers of success have anything to do with "spiritual gifts," even unconsciously, then we start to look uncomfortably like the Corinthian Christians—stuck in games of spiritual comparison. The pastor is assuming he is the most mature spiritually; the worship leader is the closest to God; the board knows what's best—because they know about money, they know how best to manage the church's finances. Paul was writing to a church like that, a church like us, more often than not.

In this kind of church, stratification of groups is almost inevitable. Well-off middle-class people go out for lunch with friends and family, while the awkward people or the people who aren't in the in-crowd go home by themselves and who knows what they do. Unfortunately, some modern church growth movements have embraced rather than resisted this natural human tendency to cluster. And some church growth might well be successfully achieved by catering to subgroups of believers who all have the same cultural preferences. With this background in mind, let's look at the details of 1 Corinthians 12.

Paul uses the image of the human body to question and probe the group dynamics going on in the church. In Paul's time this was a common way to draw attention to where the problem lies in group relations. Consider this passage from Livy, a famous historian about a generation older than Paul.

A Roman senator is trying to calm a crowd of citizens who are angry at the government. He stands before them and makes this speech:

> There was once a time when each of the parts of a man's body had its own ideas and voice. A dispute arose (like today) when the many parts began to think it unfair that they should go through all the worry and trouble to provide food for the belly, while the belly sat there quietly with nothing to do but enjoy the good things they provided for it. They conspired together that the hands should not bring food to the mouth, the mouth not accept any food, the teeth grind nothing. In this angry spirit they sought to starve the belly into submission, but while their anger burned they, and all the other body parts, grew weaker and weaker. In this way they discovered that even the belly was not idle, but also had a task to perform. By digesting and dividing what it received equally, sending it out through the blood in the veins, it nourished itself along with the other parts. Menenius Agrippa prevailed upon the minds of the hearers, having by this parallel shown the crowd how their anger at the government was like that of the dissention of the bodily members.[21]

Paul similarly needs to tackle a problem of power struggles in the Corinthian church, and the language he uses in 1 Corinthians 12:14–22 follows along the lines of Livy's.

> For in fact the body is not a single member, but many. If the foot says, "Since I am not a hand, I am not part of the body," it does not lose its membership in the body because of that. And if the ear says, "Since I am not an eye, I am not part of the body," it does not lose its membership in the body because of that. If the whole body were an eye, what part would do the hearing? If the whole were an ear, what part would exercise the sense of smell? But as a matter of fact, God has placed each of the members in the body just as he decided. If they were all the same member, where would the body be? So now there are many members, but one body. The eye cannot say to the

hand, "I do not need you," nor in turn can the head say to the foot, "I do not need you." On the contrary, those members that seem to be weaker are essential. (NET)

Even though they're both trying to intervene in what they think of as problematic group dynamics, it is crucial to see that Livy and Paul have fundamentally different pictures of what counts as healthy group dynamics.

In Livy's picture of the body, we could say that the different body parts are "cutting off their nose to spite their face." The various body parts complain with increasing bitterness that they do all the work on behalf of the stomach, while the stomach just sits there and enjoys the "fruit" of their work. They decide to quit giving the stomach food. Then everyone gets weaker because nobody is getting the nutrients they need.

Paul too confronts a situation in which people are jealous of each other's natural talents. The difference is that Livy simply assumes that all we can do in such situations is to resort to power politics. We use what power we have to coerce others into doing what we want them to do. Paul's purpose is totally different. For him the goal is to promote flourishing church life together in the Spirit. Togetherness *depends* on genuinely different people being unified in Paul's view.

The Upbuilding Power of Spiritual Gifts

Paul's goal of upbuilding the power of spiritual gifts is highlighted in the first part of 1 Corinthians 12. The chapter opens with Paul's saying that the chapter will be one in which he helps the Corinthian Christians understand the spiritual gifts. If we start with verses 4–7 and then jump to verse 11, the critical difference between Livy and Paul becomes obvious.

Now there are different gifts, but the same Spirit. And there are different ministries, but the same Lord. And there are different activities, but the same God who produces all of them in everyone. To each person the manifestation of the Spirit is given for the benefit of all. (12:4–7 NET)

It is one and the same Spirit, distributing as he decides to each person, who produces all these things. (12:11 NET)

Three key terms are interacting to make this section unique in Scripture and uniquely illuminating for thinking about the gifts of everyone in the church, including those with disabilities. The three different terms Paul uses here yield a definition of spiritual gifts that is sharply distinct from the definition of natural talents.

Paul speaks of many "gifts," "ministries," and "activities."

The first term, "gifts," is in Greek *charisma*. The term is a derivation of the verb for "giving graciously." A spiritual gift, then, is first something graciously given.

It is also a "service," which translates the Greek term *diakonia*. This term emphasizes that exercising a spiritual gift is an act of practical help. Churches sometimes have officials carrying the title "deacon." Deacons are tasked with keeping on top of the practical matters that keep a church running—that is, to serve the practical needs of the whole church. The title neatly displays the meaning of the Greek term here.

Finally, Paul says that "there are different [meaning a variety of] activities." The term he uses for "activities" is the key to his account of the gifts of the Spirit. The word "activities" is an imperfect translation of the Greek *energēma*. By using this term, Paul wants to emphasize that there is an important difference between having the power to do something and actually *doing* it.

Take an example. The sun has a lot of energy in its core that will someday be emitted as light and heat. Some of its energy, however, is already on its way to the earth. A fraction of its energy is at work at this very minute providing the light and heat that keep the earth alive (or sweating). The sun's rays that are already hitting the earth are its "activity." Paul wants to distinguish this "already actually done" power from the energy inside the sun that might, someday, emerge to warm the earth. A spiritual gift, for Paul, is something that is *actually* done, *already* done.

If we take the three terms Paul uses here together, his definition of the spiritual gifts is sparklingly clear. A spiritual gift is a work of service to another that has actually been done. If it is not these things, it is not a gift of the Holy Spirit. Being good at math or playing piano or leading a group is not a gift in itself. It all turns on how, and why, and to what effect it is used.

There's a lot of energy in the sun, but for us, all that matters are the rays that are coming down each day to keep the plants growing and the days warm. That's all that matters to Paul in defining a spiritual gift as well: that it has actually served and built up another person, specifically, another Christian.

Paul is emphatic in 1 Corinthians 12:11 that these acts of service are really the Spirit of Jesus Christ working through believers to heal and revive others. "It is one and the same Spirit, *distributing as he decides* to each person, who produces all these things" (NET). Paul goes out of his way to emphasize that the Spirit *alone* gives the gifts. In other words, Paul is explicitly excluding the sorts of natural attributes that Christians often refer to as their "gifts," such as our intelligence or our speaking skills or the abilities to achieve results we've worked so hard on.

It's probably best to call these "creational gifts." Creatures do have different capacities. Everything that God creates is filled with amazing capacities. Some have more and some have less. This is not a problem. The problem is that as sinners we tend not to know how to use those gifts, what we should do with them. When in doubt, we use them to make ourselves look better or to solidify our advantages over others. This leads to much of the infighting among Christians, as there was in Corinth in the first century.

A person might have been *created* to be a good hand or a good foot or a good bowel or a good eye in Paul's analogy, but that isn't what Paul is concerned with here. He's happy to grant that there are people that are good at different things. Instead, Paul is interested in how the Holy Spirit energizes each part to *serve the other parts*, *not* in how they function on their own. The question is how they are *empowered to build up others*. Paul is asking how the hand *serves* the foot, not how the hand functions independently. The problem is that they don't wait for one another. They want the thing that they are good at to be the most important thing. The hand is all about "bigging up" how cool it is to be a hand, not even noticing that the foot needs its shoelaces tied.

Livy uses the digestive system to show how political power struggles work when people use their created skills and social roles against one another. But Paul wants to show how the Spirit brings *unity* among very different people. How the Spirit connects people. God uses the good things that have been given to every human being for the good of the community. Spiritual gifts build up others one person at a time.

The Binding Power of Spiritual Gifts

The relationships that Paul is wanting the church to pursue can be better understood if we compare them to the nervous system. The nervous system makes it possible for body parts to work together and become one body. By giving gifts to each member, the Holy Spirit creates the nervous connections necessary for everyone to begin working together—to transmit the love that flows out from the church's head, Christ.

The gifts of the Spirit are gifts to each member of the body that allow them to serve and be in harmony with every other member. When this is happening, we together form a body that fulfills Christ's purposes.

One aspect of this new connection is that we come to experience the sufferings and joys of others in a much more direct way. "If one member suffers, all suffer together with it; if one member is honored, all rejoice together with it" (1 Cor. 12:26 NRSV).

Remember at the end of chapter 1 when I said that because my finger had been injured, I flinched when I saw a movie in which someone was smashing someone else's hand by stomping on it? I was viscerally feeling the pain of another. That was only a hint of the beautiful interconnectedness that the Spirit of Jesus Christ is striving to create in his body.

This empathetically engaged sensitivity might very well be the gift that is hardest for those of us who think we are "strong" to receive from the Spirit and to give to each other. We can certainly be helped in this by the sensitivities that often come much more easily to those with learning difficulties.

Put bluntly, if we are not a conduit of the Spirit's service to upbuild others, we are not church. We are not church because we are living out the power politics of Livy's Imperial Rome. We don't really belong to each other; we are just getting along as a matter of pragmatics. And as in Livy's parable, we really think that we are at least as important and competent and functional as every other part. This is not church—this is war.

Paul's picture is totally different. The church is that social organism that knows that it needs the different perspectives and gifts brought by very different people. It is aware that God is so big and so active that no one of us can grasp what God is doing.

We need to hear what those the world thinks of as competent have seen of the works of God. But we need even more to hear what those who are looked down on, who have to struggle to be heard, have seen of God's salvation and life-giving activity.

Paul is suggesting that one of the most telling signs by which we can identify the genuine church of Jesus Christ is that it knows the power of the Spirit that is given through those from whom society thinks there is nothing to be expected, those whom it deems weak.

Here's the point. Stop asking about people with disabilities, especially those with learning difficulties, "What are they thinking? What are they intending?" Instead, start watching what *happens* to people around them.

Don't ask, "Does Johnny with autism really understand what is going on in church?" Watch who responds when he seems to be agitated. Watch who squirms when he makes funny noises and complains to others. Who accompanies him to church? How does the pastor relate to Johnny? Such questions reveal the nervous connections that define the essence of the church—or what the church lacks.

Paul's account of the gifts of the Spirit is an elaboration of his theology of the cross, which we surveyed in chapter 3. Here he is explicitly applying it to those in the church who society has taught us have nothing to offer in the way of skills or social capital: "And on those parts of the body that we think less honorable we bestow the greater honor, and our unpresentable parts are treated with greater modesty, which our more presentable parts do not require. But God has so composed the body, giving greater honor to the part that lacked it" (1 Cor. 12:23–24 ESV). The gifts of people with disabilities are not their abilities but their acts of service. There is no church if we dismiss the gifts the Spirit gives through every human being. The cross of Jesus Christ does something to sinners. When it turns them upside down, it makes them people eager to hear something of God from those from whom society expects the least.

Receiving those gifts depends on our giving up the game of asking who has gifts and who does not. Everyone has gifts. And the Spirit wants to build up the church through every person. We miss this when we assume that only those who are obviously competent and productive are gifted. The best way to tell if we have given up this malformed question is by regularly asking ourselves if we are living up to the standard that Paul sets for empathetic engagement in the church: "Am I responsive to the joy and sorrow of others?"

Disabled in the Resurrection?

In chapter 3 I discussed Jesus's various parables about the kingdom of heaven in order to highlight the social dynamics of his kingdom on this earth. As we conclude this doctrinal chapter, we return to a question that troubles many Christians when they think about disability—the question of the resurrected body.

Many Christians with disabilities feel that the Christian assumption that everyone will be healed and made "normal" in heaven is behind the inability of Christians to believe that someone living with a disability might have come to terms with it and might not even wish to be healed of it in the resurrection.

Before we begin we must carefully note the vehemence with which Paul condemns giving this question too much weight in Christian theology, even calling a person who asks such questions a "fool" (1 Cor. 15:36 NRSV). The question of the form of the resurrected body cannot be the most important question for Christians thinking about disability. It is not the most important question because Jesus told us quite a lot about what matters in the kingdom of heaven.

We also saw in chapter 2 that disabled people themselves can have different views on this matter. Joni never wants to see a wheelchair again in heaven, while Chantal looks forward to an amazing flying wheelchair like God has in Ezekiel.

Though perhaps not the most pastorally sensitive, theologian Karl Barth's intervention saw to the theological heart of the matter. He proposed to his friend Heinrich Vogel that we need to at least be open to the idea that our resurrected bodies will be marked by the form God gave them in this life. Vogel was defending a picture of the resurrection in which all the painful limitations of this life would be totally left behind. The question was a personal one, as Vogel had a daughter with severe disabilities who had never walked. In God's new heavens and new earth, he confidently declared, "She will walk!" To Barth this smacked a little too much of charging God with having made a mistake in creating Vogel's daughter in the way God had. Vogel seemed to be asserting that God needed to make his mistake right.

> "Is it not a much more beautiful and powerful hope," Barth asked, "that something becomes apparent there that at present we cannot understand at all—namely that *this* life was not futile, because it is not in vain that God has said to it: 'I have loved: *you*!'?" And, he added, the final revelation of the truth and meaning of this life will involve a radical re-ordering of prevailing cultural values: "*She* will sit at the head of the table, while we—if we are admitted at all—will have to sit right down at the other end."[22]

These are questions about how to faithfully imagine our disabled loved one, something that every Christian parent of a special needs child must negotiate. It is a question Rachel Wright struggled with sixty years after Heinrich Vogel. "I have wondered what heaven will be like. Will Sam not be disabled, or will heaven be so inclusive and accessible that his disabilities fade into insignificance? Will I be the one who, at the gates of heaven, feels disabled having to leave my arrogance, selfishness and pride behind while Sam wheels past me without a backward glance?"[23]

The biblical warrant for thinking that Sam and people like him might not all be given bodies and minds that we think of as normal takes off from a poignant biblical detail: the fact that the resurrected Jesus still has the scars of his crucifixion (John 20:20, 25–27). Theologians through the centuries have taken this to be the central text for thinking through the form that all resurrected bodies will take.

Normate readings have typically seen the presence of the nail marks on Jesus's resurrected body as a condescension to frail humans who would not be able to recognize him otherwise. They believe that the marks on Jesus's resurrected body do not tell us anything about the constitution of resurrected bodies in general.

But even defenders of this account are forced to allow that such marks mar a resurrected body that they expect to be perfect or flawless. Many paintings, especially of "doubting" Thomas probing Jesus's scars, have lodged a picture in Christians' minds of Jesus's resurrected body still having open wounds.

But the biblical text in John just uses the more neutral term "marks." It is unlikely that John was imagining Jesus, the great healer, having overcome death but not having had his wounds heal or at least close up. One thing can be said for certain: Jesus's resurrected body is not one that is entirely cleansed of everything that we might think of as defects. His skin, at least, is not scar-free.

This is a crucial admission, because the scars that remain are ones that were made at the most difficult and painful part of Jesus's life. The marks of his disabling experience on the cross are not cleansed from his resurrected body—they are transfigured and made glorious.

Indeed, it was commonly assumed in the ancient world that people would be recognizable in the afterlife *because* of their scars. It was also presumed that different scars had different moral valances. The scar on the neck of a soldier killed in battle was considered more honorable than the scars on the back of an enslaved person from enduring the whip.[24] John's first readers would have therefore seen Jesus's resurrection scars as badges of honor in displaying his glorious victory over Satan and Caesar's worst defeat.

The idea that we will be resurrected in conformity with a perfect human form came into the church with Neoplatonist theologies like that of Augustine, who struggled mightily with how Jesus could have been resurrected with apparent imperfections.[25] This metaphysical overlay has obscured the plain sense of Scripture, which affirms that we will not lose all bodily particularity in the resurrection.[26]

Disabled people need not fear being made unrecognizable in the healing of the resurrection. Nor should those without disabilities imagine that every disabled person wishes to be resurrected in what nondisabled people assume to be the "normal" human body. But does that mean that in the resurrection disabilities will still be present, which entails certain body parts are not functional? That Chantal will still have legs but not the use of them for walking? This seems an odd thought.

Once again, however, the thought is clearly present in the Bible. In Mark 12:19–25 Jesus suggests that people will be resurrected male and female but "like the angels"—that is, not engaging in reproduction. To be a man or a woman in the resurrection will mean having parts that will not function reproductively. So in Jesus's anthropology, it seems that every body part does not have to have a function in order to be beautiful and good.

Augustine is closer to Scripture than most modern Christians' assumptions about resurrection bodies in being prepared to consider that bodies with nonfunctioning parts might actually be more beautiful than ones in which the only things that remain are functioning parts. A woman and a man who will not reproduce in heaven but who have all their sexual characteristics removed would be *less* beautiful if they lost these nonfunctioning parts.[27]

This is not to flatly claim that functioning will definitely not be restored to bodies in the resurrection. It is instead to insist that Jesus is at least allowing that the restoration of function as we imagine it is not what matters about resurrection integrity and functionality. The normate obsession with functionality may be skewing how we imagine the resurrection.

Here's a really radical set of thoughts. A church that has learned the beauty of the diversity of Christ's body will have learned to see the beauty in all kinds of people's bodies. Not because they are just looking at bodies but because they have learned to cherish the gifts that God has given through each person. To be church is therefore to be amazed by the bodies that God has used for his amazing purposes on this earth. We won't want to forget what we learned from Chantal and Joni, and we won't want the bodies that made them so memorable entirely erased, as Jesus's scars were not erased. We'll be looking forward to a heaven full of diversely beautiful bodies that cause no one pain and that do not divide us from one another. Bodies and minds that today some find repulsive will be gloriously visible to all in the beauty that God's eyes behold in them.

I am trying to draw attention to the spiritual implications of our assumptions about church. Do we think that people who have been burned or who don't dress well or who drool on their clothes don't really "fit" at church? To the extent that we experience people as repellant to our views of beauty, it is our views of beauty that are misshapen.

We will be resurrected to the beauty that God sees in us, not according to the standards of beauty of our age. What a relief.

FIVE

We Don't Know Where to Start

Most Christians want to be welcoming of anyone who comes to church. But when it comes to disability, Christians often find themselves not knowing what to do. Not knowing what to say. Fear of doing the wrong thing makes it easy not to do anything. This is a story we have heard often throughout this book. To make sure we are clear about the practical problem in this chapter, a story from Ben Conner should clarify just what is at stake.

Ben takes his friend Meghan to church every week. Meghan has cerebral palsy and is mobile, but she "has difficulty communicating verbally and knows it, so in an effort to make sure you can understand what she is saying, she tends to say things at least twice." Meghan has a job, goes horseback riding once a week at a therapeutic riding center, and regularly texts her friends, using emojis that correspond to her mood or what she is doing.

> On the weekends, she joins my family at church (and texts us an emoji of a church to let us know she is there and waiting for us), and she is an important part of our community of witness. Though she can't read, she participates in all aspects of the worship service and offers habituated responses to the music and the recitation of the Apostles' Creed. Meghan has a contagious enthusiasm about church and emits a profoundly joyful and largely nonverbal witness to being included

in the body of Christ. . . . One Sunday when we were out of town, Meghan attended church by herself. She sat in the balcony where we often sit together. No one sat close to her. During the songs, no one found the correct pages in the hymnal for her. At some point during the service, her phone began to buzz, and she was unable to turn it off. People around her "shushed" her and looked at her in a way that she interpreted as harsh and angry. No one helped her. She began to cry. No one comforted her. She quickly left the church, ran home, and cried.[1]

Conner comments, "It should be obvious that Meghan is not suffering because of her cerebral palsy or limited intellectual development. In fact, she is generally one of the most joyful people I know. She does, however, suffer when she feels unwelcomed, excluded, or like she doesn't belong. Don't we all?"[2]

I hope that by now it has become clear that becoming a church that is not threatened by disability experiences is no more complicated than seeing that this is the problem. Because Christians feel awkward about disability, churches become places in which disabled people feel unwelcome. This is also an example of the "hesitation blues."[3] We are often unconscious of what our body language and facial expressions are communicating. Meghan probably knew this congregation better than it knows itself. Christians are often trapped by the hesitation blues—sure that we should engage with someone but unsure how to do so and afraid of doing the wrong thing. Fear is our enemy. Not knowing what to do is our enemy. And "the way we have always done it" is our enemy.

This final chapter suggests what the church looks like that "gets it." It attempts to describe a church that has learned that disability is not threatening but promising. Disability is a promise of new life in such an unexpected package that we don't know how to receive it.

Welcome Takes a Whole Church

The approach taken in this book assumes that everything follows from *seeing* what's at stake. A good heart is not enough. Knowing the Bible is not enough. Setting up a "special needs" ministry is not enough. The whole church needs to become more aware of—and embrace—the sheer diversity of human life if our best intentions are not to play out in hurtful actions.

Catherine Webb might not seem like your average person with a disability experience. She is a certified speech and language pathologist and is working on her doctorate in disability studies. Her disabilities are invisible, chronic pain and a diagnosed anxiety disorder that has roots in her brain makeup. Catherine's anxiety can be medicated but not eradicated, given its basis in her brain chemistry. Her chronic pain is likewise something attached to her bodily limits that can be treated in various ways, but it will never go away. Her professional and academic experiences have also allowed her to see the stigmas that often surround mental illness and neurodiversity. This makes her reticent to reveal her anxiety to people in church, though she does tell people she trusts about her chronic pain. However, she finds the labor of putting on a brave face and trying to appear "normal" emotionally taxing.

Being at church is thus a fraught experience for Catherine, one in which she must carefully decide when to speak truthfully about her challenges and some of the most important aspects of her faith. It is also a context in which people who do not know her disability experience express thoughts that directly assault Catherine's assurance that she is a good creature made by God. Unfortunately, this is not a rare experience. One instance in particular continues to haunt her. It happened in the intimacy of a home Bible study

> with some very nice people, many of whom were raised in the church and whom I genuinely like. As we read and discussed a book together, we ended up talking about anxiety. The conversation progressed and people began expressing how all anxiety is sin and needs to be repented of and, therefore, stopped and not re-experienced. I asked people to consider how there is a difference between everyday anxiety and chronic anxiety, and was summarily dismissed. I was essentially told, "It says in the Bible not to be anxious, so all anxiety is sinful, and a constant state of sinning separates you from God. Period."
>
> I left Bible study that night knowing I could never be myself with the people who were a part of that group and that it was not a welcoming place for me to grow in my faith. It also sent me into a thought

spiral: "If who I am at my core, who I was biologically made to be, is permanently separated from God because of how He made me, then how do I deepen or even have faith? If there is no hope for me, ever, because my genes won't let me repent forever and stop being anxious, then why would God make me this way?" These thoughts were not intentionally expressed by the group to hurt me, but the implicit beliefs behind their statements created in me a deep, painful knowledge that I cannot be loved or accepted for who I am.[4]

This story makes plain why there can be no single prescription on how to become a healing and welcoming church. The hurt in this story arises from the combination of unawareness of certain kinds of disabilities and a wooden, literalist reading of Scripture.

The hurt caused to Meghan in the first story in this chapter was different. It sprang from expectations about appropriate behavior in church combining in a noxious way with the hesitation blues that people expressed when Meghan seemed to be doing something awkward.

Disability presents the church with such different types of challenges that it threatens to be immobilizing. But it doesn't have to be. As we've seen, it can actually be very simple: "Wait for one another." But what does that mean?

One thing we can assume on the basis of the discussion of the spiritual gifts in chapter 4 is that every local church has what it needs to be welcoming. It has its own unique identity and ways of living out the gospel. Things that fit well in one community may not work in another. That's why our churches won't get going on disability-related issues until we all begin to see the problem. Then we can learn a few simple first steps to practice when we see the problem arising.

It's Not about a Program

Notice I did not say what many church leaders will be expecting (and perhaps even secretly hoping) to hear: "You need to set up a disability ministry." Instead, I said that the *whole* church needs to begin to wait for one another. Paul's prescription on this point was not and indeed cannot be just for church leaders (see 1 Cor. 11:17–34 and my discussion of these verses in chap. 3). It works only if the whole church is involved.

Church leaders are tempted to set up a separate disability ministry because it means they can turn "the problem" over to experts. Sometimes this can end up meaning a long delay while the church tries to find an expert. Other times, especially in bigger, richer churches, this can mean that a disability minister is hired and separate services are begun that cater to those with special needs.

Sarah Shae and Sam Ip are pastors in a disability ministry at a large evangelical church in Hong Kong. Most of the people who attend their ministry live in a sheltered housing complex in a nearby high-rise apartment building. For many of them, this trip to church is their only trip out of that building all week.

But the special needs ministry, though well supported, meets in a separate building from the main church. For years Sarah and Sam have been trying to persuade the church that they need their disabled brothers and sisters with them. But they have not been able to overcome the congregation's resistance to worshiping together.

This may be an extreme case, but it is not untypical. Churches can imagine ministering *to* people with disabilities but find it much harder to understand themselves as worshiping *with* people with disabilities—especially intellectual disabilities.

While having a disability ministry is certainly better than not engaging with the disability experience at all, such ministries necessarily fall short of the vision of church Paul is holding out to us. He does not say, "Set up a place where the slower people can do things at their own pace." He says to the *whole* church, "Wait for one another."

Those who aspire to church leadership have rarely gotten there by waiting for one another. So this is a hard message to hear. It is much easier to set up a program and let the specialists deal with it.

Once churches have programs, they have to fit people into them. And the rest of the congregation can proceed as if the "problem" of disability is resolved.

It's much harder to preach on this theme, let alone let someone with disabilities preach on this theme—or even be put on the pastoral staff. But this yearning for unity in real diversity is what church is, fundamentally. The unity of the church in diversity remains the essence of the church even if the ways most of us think about being "leadership material" hide this truth.

It is important not to leave readers with the sense that no good work is done in the many high-quality special needs ministries that have sprung up over the last decade. Often such ministries do serve some people with disabilities well, and when they do, they inevitably draw in more as word spreads.

If you have a ministry in your church, and it is working, Amen! Any church that manages to make a welcoming and secure space for those with disabilities and their families to meet is to be commended. At the same time, it is important to ask the questions I have raised in this section about how well those being ministered to are integrated into the whole life of the congregation. Something vital is lost if all members of a congregation do not have opportunities to get to know and receive the gifts of people with special needs in their church. We have to be able to discern the difference between a ministry that solves a "problem" for a congregation and the comprehensive vision of mutual interdependence offered in the New Testament.

Church Is Not School

There is also a more practical reason to try to avoid setting up separate special needs services. Most of the guidebooks for churches about how to set up a special ministry replace theological language with the language and goals of social services and special education. Once we've set things up this way, Fox observes, "it is no wonder that the practices of public schools and secular services become the template for church practices regarding people with developmental disabilities."[5]

It is good for Christians to learn what they can from special education and social services literature and to learn the special terminology used in them. But when churches have no other language to describe what they are doing, something critical is lost. That something critical is, first, the engagement of the *whole* congregation and, second, the loss of the church's capacity to think creatively within its own most fertile and life-giving language and stories.

Church is not school. Nor is it a social services provider. It can draw on and learn from the best practices of these institutionalized forms of care for people with disabilities. It is good that it does so. Yet something is drastically wrong when Christians see themselves as constantly having to catch up to the welcome provided by secular public agencies, Fox concludes. "Without our practices being grounded in faith, the essential transformative element is missing. Our *how* of welcoming people with developmental disabilities into every aspect of church life must be deeply connected to our professed *why*: our faith in Jesus Christ."[6]

The first question that should come into Christians' minds when someone with a disability comes into church should not be "What are we going to need to do to adapt to them?" That this is so often the case is a sign that Christians have not yet grasped that the question of disability is really a question about how broad and diverse we are imagining the body of Christ to be.

Churches have all too often seen discipleship as a process of helping people conform to the social codes that have been set up in order to achieve an "appropriate" worship experience. Jeff McNair is the founder of Reality Ministries in Durham, North Carolina. For over a dozen years he has run weekly campus-ministry-style events for young adults with learning impairments. As fun as such ministries can be, he suggests that they are also an indictment of most churches that "not only reflect normality [but] enforce normality, in a relatively constrained way. That is, it doesn't take much in terms of difference for you to stand out at church."[7]

Most of our churches are configured in social-skill intensive ways. There are a lot of social cues to be learned, and people who come are expected to step up and join in. Amy Jacober tells a story about a conflict at school in which people display an unwillingness to alter even the simplest habitual patterns, which surprises few parents who have taken a disabled child to church.

> My daughter has a friend in her class who has a host of severe allergies. At the tender age of five, Allison had to address this with her entire kindergarten class. Allison's parents sent a letter home to the parents of other children in her class, asking that certain foods not

be included in lunches. Quite reasonably, Allison's parents said that, if parents wanted to include some of those foods in their children's lunch, they requested that the child simply eat lunch in the other classroom and rejoin his or her classmates afterwards. One mother refused to comply. She made a very public statement about how this infringed on her rights and that these allergies were all a hoax. Allison's response was astonishing. She was so concerned that the girl whose mother refused to comply would feel isolated, left out, or be teased that she asked if she, that is Allison herself, could sit a table alone for every lunch so that she needn't fear an anaphylactic episode and that the other girl could be with her friends. When I asked her why she did that, she simply said because Jesus calls us to be kind even when others aren't. God revealed himself to her and, in what seemed like a mundane daily task, even a five year old is compelled to respond. That is worship.[8]

What does it look like to wait for one another? It at least means being prepared to seriously ask how we might configure our corporate gatherings so that nonconformity is not immediately labeled a disruption. That's waiting for one another. To actually want people to be with us, even if we have to change. To have the Holy Spirit's desire for us to be together overwhelm our feelings of awkward embarrassment.

The Language Problem

It is terribly sad that the culture wars around politically correct language have set up barriers to Christian communion. We no longer know if we should refer to the obvious or if we should avoid mentioning it. We don't even know what to call "it."

So we hesitate. Then we feel bad about hesitating, not least because we know the other person knows we feel awkward. This is the hesitation blues, and most churches have it bad.

There are good reasons to be nervous in this territory. Labeling people always puts them in a group, and people often don't like the group they've been put in.

I learned this the hard way when I was about twelve years old, in junior high. I went to a very racially stratified school, with lots of different kinds of minority students. At lunch one day, a white boy with whom I was casually acquainted was sitting with a Hispanic boy. As I walked by, I made a comment that I thought was applying a label innocently. "I didn't know you were a lowrider now." Every racial group had its label, of course, and I had a big mouth—in my no doubt self-serving memory, I was just saying what came into my head, which was surprise at this breach of racial convention.

It doesn't really matter what I meant by it, in the end. On the playground outside fifteen minutes later, I felt a tap on my shoulder, and my first full-on punch in the nose. It was the Hispanic boy from the lunch table. Clearly the label hurt. I'm glad now for that lesson, as painful as it was at the time. I was wrong to have carved the world up into racial groupings as I did. How was I to learn how wrong I was without any honest feedback? Though not exactly eloquent, a fist does honestly reveal the truth of the pain I had caused.

The problem is that people feel they have to be polite at church, so if a label hurts, it is usually the one who feels mislabeled who takes the punch. And never comes back. It's important, then, that we Christians figure out how to get our language right. There's really only one contemporary debate on this topic worth knowing about, the debate about "person first" language.

The debate has to do with whether we say, "Jane is a person with autism" or "Jane is autistic."

The truth is, there are few hard-and-fast rules here. It is generally safe to say that both Deaf people who use sign language and autistic people prefer not to use a label that suggests that they are a person separable from their condition. They are proud of what they have achieved and who they are, and many find the suggestion that they are somehow a "person" separable from these traits off-putting. Some do not like these conditions to be labeled disabilities at all.

In general, it is therefore best in one-on-one conversations to simply ask someone's name and use it. Use eye contact and gentle touch with nonverbal people. We don't really need a label for most conversations.

We do need a label when we are talking to a larger group, however. We've surveyed some of the theological problems with the label "disability" (most obviously, the designation of a group of people as *unable* to do things), but it remains the commonly accepted label.

If a pastor wants to preach a sermon or write to a lot of people (as I have in this book), it is hard to avoid using the term "disability" to direct attention to the disability experience more broadly. For those who want to address these issues, I would suggest keeping in mind the issues I raised in chapter 1: the disability experience is very often more complex and more widespread than we think. In the end, however, it is the tonality behind whatever language we use that matters most. Remember, Christians are to be like Philip, running alongside those God is drawing into his community.

Christians need to be ready to sit down alongside the Ethiopian eunuch, saying with him that we cannot understand unless we let people tell us about themselves when they are ready. When they do, we need to follow their cues to describe their condition in the terms *they* choose.

Language is important but respect is even more so. And a willingness to listen and learn is one of the greatest indicators of respect.

Churches cannot avoid sitting with the fact that we have seen our role in discipleship as *training* people in the language of faith and worship. Aside from the tiny number of missionary Bible translators, Christians have very often not been good at *learning other people's languages*, observes Amy Jacober. "Most of us need to be encouraged to listen differently. If we take the time to listen, voices from the marginalized edges of society are not only present, they are deafening. They can be missed, blending in with the white noise of our world. Yet their voices are there, clear and present."[9]

Jacober's point makes sense only when we realize how much communication is always taking place nonverbally. This is true of all of us, all the time. We only know what people mean when they say "I'm fine" by looking at all kinds of nonverbal cues. Sometimes people mean it, and other times their body language and tone plead with us to ask for more: "Really?"

Rebecca Spurrier spent five years studying and worshiping with a church in Atlanta called Sacred Family Church, which had a high percentage of learning-impaired congregants. After having puzzled through the characteristic patterns of communication in this congregation, she discovered that learning the languages of people with disabilities is often a matter of taking the time to see their communication in the context of other activities.

Albie attends Sacred Family Church and has special needs. He is known for sitting silently and alone. Ben, a church intern, tries to reach out.

> Albie was playing with a chess board, and Ben wanted to play with him, so he [Ben] said, "Can I set up the board, the normal way?" and Ben made his opening move, and Albie made his opening move, and it came into being that Albie would just kind of move [a chess piece] in a way that didn't have anything to do with the rules of chess. Ben was going along with it, trying to figure out what he [Albie] was trying to do, so he finally ended up . . . [with] Albie [taking] almost all of Ben's pieces off the board, and the change that Ben described [as] from "we're going to have a game" to "oh I'm gonna try to figure out what's going on with him, what does he want with this [game]?"[10]

The game has morphed into a medium of communion and communication. Winning and losing has become no more than a way station to getting to know one another, concludes Spurrier. "Perhaps the whole point of the game is that Albie wants to win a game of chess on his own terms, but Albie also initiates a repartee by which the two can play and in which the intern, the newcomer to the community, does not control the game in a normal way. Ben is not the teacher of a game Albie cannot play. Rather than either of them telling the other how to play, Albie moves pieces around a board, allowing nonverbal dialogue on the board to unfold between them."[11]

That's why the story of the Ethiopian eunuch is so powerful. Philip never imagined that the gospel would go as far as Africa or draw in such different kinds of people!

When we see others whom we don't know how to label and whose way of speaking we find very hard to understand, we have to see such moments as leading us out to grasp the depth of our own tradition better and more deeply.

The church *needs* diversity in order for Christians to perceive the depth of the gospel we confess. That gospel is for the whole world, even if we have tried to narrow it to the groups of people and practices that make us most comfortable.

Philip had to *run* after the Ethiopian eunuch. It cost him some sweat (and that terribly embarrassing sound of flapping sandals!). That's what it took to follow the Spirit that blows where it wills.

Beyond the Hesitation Blues

Let's get down to the nuts and bolts. Recall the discussion, which opened chapter 4, about where people in churches often start thinking about disability—with disability as a tragic effect of the fall. We saw how that starting point sets up the first interaction with people with disabilities all wrong. Starting from here, Christians have nothing positive to say to someone living a disability experience. Next come the hesitation blues. Not knowing what to say, we look at the floor or drift in a different direction.

Let's be honest, we've been there. Let's start over from a different theological starting point. The work of the Holy Spirit of Jesus Christ can be counted on to draw together people who do not normally interact. Philip's engagement with the Ethiopian eunuch is a prime example of what this looks like. The Holy Spirit is also the tractor beam drawing people into a living organism made up of empathetic connections and works of service to one another. That organism is the body of Christ. Finally, everything God weaves together in the human womb is good.

These are the three theological claims we need to have in mind in order to be ready to interact with anyone with special needs. We need to inhabit these theological affirmations, not just in word but in deed, in the way we carry ourselves.

We also have to keep in mind a crucial sociological fact. People with disabilities, or people with disabilities in their families, are constantly battling the status quo. Nothing in society is arranged in a way that makes things easy for them.

They have to book a wheelchair taxi to get to church. They have to go through a laborious morning dressing, eating, and toileting routine. Trying something that diverges from previous patterns may provoke loud and embarrassing emotional meltdowns.

As one parent of a special needs child has observed, with every one of these external struggles comes its parallel, and exhausting, inner struggle.

> As the parent of a child with complex needs, much of what I find difficult in dealing with the challenges of life is tied up in how I see everyone else. Such disparity between my life and others' supercharges the teenager in me, screaming, "It's not fair!" If left in my own little bubble, with no apparent "standard" to set myself against, things might be quite different. If, as a first time mum, I only had Sam as a marker, I could have easily celebrated his smile, joy and thick, squidgy wrists. But when I looked at my friends' children, my heart sank. They were grasping and looking, then sitting and rolling. Against their backdrop of galloping through milestones, Sam was missing out. With these comparisons, I felt a piercing sense of disappointment. Circumstances can be tough, but when you throw in comparison, it's like gasoline on the flame.[12]

This is a useful reminder that the pressing experience of disability may be that of people who actually have a disabling condition. Often, however, it will be those who live with and love them who are on their last legs when they arrive at the church door.

For all these reasons, people with disabilities and those who live with and love them need to be assumed to be arriving at the church door with little patience or initiative left. They will need to be lovingly shown that they are genuinely welcomed, not just tolerated.

Now we come to the interesting point, and this one requires a lot on both sides. Christians all too often believe that church is a place where we have to dress up and be well behaved. I haven't met the family yet that has not experienced a stony silence on the way to church after having fought or pushed to get everyone dressed up and ready to go on time. But when we get to church, we put on a smile (most of the time). We do that because we think church is a place where we act like we have it all together.

In short, Christians pretty much see church as a place where we *hide* our needs and weaknesses. No wonder we are so unwound when someone appears who seems needy, who might, God forbid, need some assistance not only in the toilet but even getting to the toilet.

The Magic Moment

I believe that the breakthrough into the workspace of the Spirit comes in that magic moment when someone lets their need or discomfort show and people respond. This is the place of real transformation.

Churches will need to remember that it will not be easy for people wrestling with disability experiences to ask for help. Many times families are simply too tired to risk another rejection or even to try to explain what is going on, as Joe Landis notes. "Families who have members with disabilities, for their part, are often so overwhelmed with the challenges of advocating for a loved one that they have little strength or initiative left to reach out to the faith community. They believe, as parents have told me in the past, 'Church is not a place to put yourself forward, burden others, or complain.' And so, not out of hesitation or bad intention, the hesitation blues continue, and both parties go off in separate directions."[13]

What is true in every case of a family that has someone with disabilities in it, is that trying to be present with them and to love them well has meant costly energy expenditure doing all sorts of things that come easily and quickly to others. To stop covering up our needs and discomforts is an expression of the desire of every human heart to be joined together, to belong to one another. This is the precarious, vulnerable moment from which new life sprouts.

> There are a lot of reasons why we as a family struggle to accept help. It may be the intrusion of privacy, or concern that others may not be doing it "right". There can also be a deep feeling of failure, or the belief that we "should be able to do this on our own". A big one is pride. Accepting help may in some way offend our ego. It can be painfully humbling to be dependent on others. But these barriers to accepting help all crumble when we learn to let go of the myth of independence. None of us are or should ever be independent. God created us for community, and we are missing out on something if independence is our goal. Moses' supernatural (God-given) power influencing the battle at Rephidim was dependent upon him raising his staff. When his arms got tired, he sat down and let his friends support him. . . . Community has to be a two-way street. The walls of fear and pride, erected to protect our independence, are unhelpful and ungodly. If we

let our guard down, allowing people to help with life's burdens, we open ourselves up to experiencing a depth of God's love only tasted through vulnerability and interdependence.[14]

The beautiful thing is that need and confusion can be expressed from either side of an interchange. It is true that some people with disabilities can tell us what they want. But putting the onus on them to do so looks an awful lot like putting another burden on them.

The reality is that there would not be a "problem of disability" in our churches if church people would be willing to expose their ignorance and say, "I'm really sorry, but I can't understand what you are saying, could you repeat that?" Or, "Your child seems distressed and I'm not sure how I can help. Is there any way we can make it better for her?" Or, "I'm so embarrassed that I responded badly and didn't see you needed a hand. Can I sit with you?" Christians need to be brave enough as disciples to risk the vulnerability of saying, "I don't know what to do here."

Congregants will need to sensitively discern when the time is right to reach out. The key thing to get across in every register possible is this message: "We're not sure how to do this, but let us figure it out *with* you." It is a message that conveys, "We're glad you're here. You belong." Use the words that feel right to you, but this is what needs to come through loud and clear.[15]

From here on out, it's all trial and error. That's why making sure people hear that we want to figure it out together is so crucial. We need to be so convincing from the outset that we invite trust to be born.

Trial and Error

Trial and error is the only way forward because the range of disability experiences is so broad, as the many stories in this book have illustrated. Not only are disabilities vastly varied, but they often develop over time. The responses of people wrestling with these experiences also develop over time. Welcoming and supporting people through disability experiences will always need to be context sensitive. It will also necessarily need to evolve over time.

The beautiful thing about a trial-and-error process is that it becomes a crucible in which trust, then respect, and finally friendship
can grow. Relationships form in which people become aware of what
they have been given by God *from each other*. As the charity model
of Christians doing "good deeds" for "needy people" gives way to
relationship, trust emerges out of the business of negotiating daily
issues.

In the process expectations are turned upside down. *We* thought
we were helping *them*, but we find ourselves receiving more than we've
given. Because we have built a relationship over time, we discover that
those we expected very little from turn out to have amazing insights
or speak a word to us in such an uncanny way that we cannot avoid
believing it has come straight from God, as Amy Jacober found out
when accompanying a group of disabled teenage girls in a church
youth group. Her story begins when picking up a new girl at school
before the group's first gathering.

> "This is Susie," the teacher announced. I looked into her eyes and
> said warmly, "Hi, Susie." No response. Instinctively, I suspected that
> Susie was autistic. A common misconception about individuals with
> autism is that nothing gets through to them. In reality, it is just the
> opposite. Everything gets through to them as if the volume were set
> to ten. The effect is that an autistic person shuts down to filter out the
> overwhelming stimulation coming through their senses.
>
> So reading Susie was next to impossible over the next few weeks
> as she continued to join us. Was she having a good time? Did she like
> being there? What was going on in her private world? Many times Susie
> would stand and gently rock herself with a blank expression. I would
> look hoping to see what was going on behind her sherry-colored eyes,
> but I could discern nothing. I longed to make some kind of connec-
> tion with her. When I touched her hand to lead her to sit down, she
> would pull it back as if it had been burned. In spite of this apparent
> lack of connection to anyone during youth group, she continued to
> come week after week.[16]

It is worth pausing to notice that Jacober initially felt significant
lack of clarity about what was happening with Susie, how to make
a connection. But Jacober felt desire for that connection, and she

began actively to seek it. She did not let her sense of confusion lead her to abandon being present to Susie in a nondemanding way. Slowly, Susie opened up.

> That summer, surprisingly, Susie signed up for [summer] camp. In order to attend, she would need someone to be with her around the clock. A wonderful high school sophomore named Ashley volunteered to be Susie's guide, friend, and attendant for the week. Ashley had been to camp earlier that summer and had given her life to Christ. She jumped at the opportunity to give back out of her new relationship with him and others. It would be a costly, sacrificial act of service and kindness. There would be very little free time, if any. Ashley would have to attend to Susie's every need. She would be responsible to help her integrate into the life of the camp, meet other kids who would likely be afraid and avoid her. She would have to help her eat, dress, and take her to the restroom. Ashley would be Susie's secure point of contact in a frightening and unknown world. [17]

The perseverance of both Jacober and Susie to be present in church was beginning to lead to the weaving of wider circles of bonding and trust. The new disciple Ashley discovers her own call to trust the leading of the Spirit of Jesus and spend her week with Suzie. She too will have her feelings of confusion and frustration during this week. But also joy.

> The middle of the week brought a Western hoedown. Susie let Ashley lead her in dancing. She followed Ashley and the rest of the campers and seemed to be connecting with the joy and movement of dance. As the dance ended Ashley led Susie over to the basketball bleachers to rest along with two other leaders, Lydia and Shelley. Caught up in the fun spirit of the evening, I headed over to join them. When I reached them, I broke out into a spontaneous silly dance while singing at the top of my lungs. Shelly interrupted me and whispered, "[Amy], look at Susie." I turned and witnessed a wonder—a God moment. Susie was rocking herself, but instead of staring vacantly, both sides of her mouth were curled up in a smile. Her eyes were sparkling with silent mirth as she was looking at me. I was caught completely off guard and stood speechless, smiling right back. Inwardly, I was overcome with awe. It appeared to be an ordinary and

insignificant moment, but I knew I stood in the presence of God who lived behind Susie's eyes, and for that instant had brought her out to play.[18]

In moments like these, those from whom we expect very little image Christ's face smiling upon us. This is why, for Christians, disability is not just one topic among others. What the least of these have done unto us, Christ has done unto us.

Becoming a Community of Reconciliation

Changing habits as deep as the ones that have been the focus of this book is not easy. The us-and-them line of demarcation that divides "the disabled" from "normal" people implicates many habits of mind, heart, body, and social interaction. Courage and perseverance will be needed to begin to make new moves since the habits of mind and social practices that keep us separated from one another are often unconsciously held.

It is all too easy for conflicts to arise in churches as they try to become more welcoming to people with various disabilities. The reasons are many.

People who suffer with mental illness find it taxing to engage with people who have never encountered it.

People with disabilities often do not have much money and usually earn little. They often rely on the support of those who do have money and may randomly ask people they meet for money.

Few churches appoint people with special needs to their leadership teams or committees. Thus church practices of leadership and administration often not-too-subtly entrench the divisions between the "competent" and the "incompetent."

Events that are organized to cater to the relatively wealthy and able are often not enjoyable to those who have learning difficulties or who live in care homes—leading to groups naturally divided according to status.

And many people with special needs simply live according to different rhythms of life, having reasons for doing things that seem odd, difficult, or initially off-putting to many congregants.

Jack, a middle-aged white man living in a group home in Atlanta, told this story of his first encounters with Sacred Family Church. When asked why he was attracted to the church, he replied,

> This is a church that is doing what the church is actually supposed to do, and that is reaching out to people with disabilities, whether they be mental or physical, and to become an intricate part of the community, and that's what they are to me. And I admit, when I first came—I still use tobacco—and I came just to eat and smoke because I was hungry. But after coming for a while and . . . seeing what was going on around me, I started asking questions, and before you know it, I was a part of the church. But there are people who come just to eat and smoke.

"Is that alright, you think?" asks the interviewer, Rebecca Spurrier. "Yeah, that's alright. That was me for a couple of months."[19]

It is not difficult to imagine the sorts of conflicts that might emerge if someone like Jack were to show up in most churches today. He might raise questions about appropriate lifestyles, about appropriate dress and behavior, about appropriate language, about appropriate dress. He might be hard to integrate into Sunday school groups or to include in church outings or board meetings. Jack, like everyone else, is still a human being and a sinner, and so he is very likely to be as selfish as the rest of us, intermittently not sure why he is there and liable to going somewhere else where the swag seems better.

Yet his challenge stands: "This is a church that is doing what the church is actually supposed to do." His challenge is difficult to evade. It is also difficult to live out for those who do not want to put their head in the sand about the reality of disability.

And yet, "Wait for one another," says Paul. Share in one another's joys and griefs. Love people through their lows, their confusions, and their off-putting habits.

It also helps to keep in mind that most adults with special needs who have been through state institutions of care have had to face being labeled "noncompliant" or "manipulative" when they have refused to conform to the expectations of those looking after them.

The "challenging behaviors" they may have developed might be rational responses to inhumane care systems. Emotional outbursts, physical and verbal aggression, disruptive vocal and physical behaviors, property destruction, self-injury, and withdrawal are all behaviors that make total sense when we imagine a lifetime spent in near incarceration for those without the mental capacity to think through the wider context of their situation. The tragedy, notes Bill Gaventa, is that "whatever the types of behavior and wherever they happen, challenging behaviors are often ones that confound, frustrate, and anger family members, caregivers, and peers. Far too often, the end results are that the person with the behavior first gets blamed without taking the context into account, and, second, the power dynamics of trying to gain control ratchets up on both sides, often leading to punishment, isolation, or exclusion (or worse), with no one pleased about the outcome."[20]

The challenge is to be a church that has intentionally built the capacity to absorb such behaviors while letting people know that they are loved.

Becoming a Community of Hope

A church that is learning to love in the face of what it experiences as awkwardness and disruption becomes a place where hope can spring up. Churches allow people the security and support to become more at peace with themselves as they become more embedded in relationship. A community of mutually upbuilding service heals because it allows people, perhaps for the first time, to hope.

There will be challenges being a church that opens its hearts to the fullness of human life. But those who embrace its challenge very often find new life, as Fiona, a white middle-class woman who attends Jack's church, recounts. When asked what captured her about a church with so many awkward angles, a church that took work to be part of, Fiona replied that after her initial shock and surprise subsided, she found life in the community captivating:

> This is the experience of coming to Sacred Family. . . . The very worst thing that could ever happen to me, to be homeless and to lose my mind—that would be my deepest fear of my universe. . . . And then you come here, and that's what this is, and I meet my fear, right there in my face, raw, staring back at me, touching me, looking at me,

doing the hokey-pokey with me at the dance . . . because that was
the first thing it was, a dance. That was my deepest fear, and then
you settle into it and you take a breath. . . . That's what captured me
and hooked me. And the fear hasn't gone but . . . even from that first
dance, it was fun. . . . And I kept coming back, learning, and just
being really interested, and interested in mental illness and poverty
and learning about my friends here. . . . I'm kind of embarrassed.
This could be anybody. This could be my brother. This could be me.
These are just my family here that suffers from severe mental illness
and poverty. From where I sit, I often think, you know, what I have
are resources and a support network that keeps me tethered to my
bubble and my village, but it's real, I believe passionately, for all of
us, fragile, and if you become ill and/or your resource network goes,
anybody could be here. You could come from any walk of life. This
could be me.[21]

Embracing disability will provoke our deepest anxieties. It will
bring out the disdain we have for others of which we are not even
aware. It will show us our disdain for parts of our own bodies we
find repellant. It will show us our fears.

Combating all these forces will take work, hard work. Yet because it is kingdom work, in it Christians discover they are made
for one another, can have fun together, and will not be swallowed
by joining one another's pain. And with these will also come new
experiences of joy, because, as Fiona observed, "These are just my
family here." At the same time, it will lead to a more vibrant church,
to people with and without disabilities having a clearer sense of
their vocations and the grandeur of their place in God's story with
the world. It will mean the transfiguration of painful wounds into
glorious scars.

Churches that have learned to welcome disability will have the
privilege of seeing emotional pain and psychological illness soothed
and personalities flower.

Becoming a Community of Discernment

Alice Teisan was an active, Christian, single woman in the prime of
her life. She was also a trained nurse heavily involved in a Christian

sports youth ministry. It was therefore immensely distressing when she was stricken by a debilitating disease that left her listless and in constant pain. She found herself reduced to sleeping all the time and hardly able to think straight. The condition lasted for months, then for a year, all the time eluding diagnosis. She had to quit her ministry. Work became impossible.

Seven years after the onset of this unnamed disability, insurance investigators began clandestinely to build a case against her. They succeeded in terminating her insurance on the grounds that she was not really disabled. Alice was abruptly thrown into a life of fighting for financial survival. As a nurse, she had been trained in filling out paperwork, but now that was all that was keeping her alive.

Economizing was to become her new way of life without any means of financial support. She sold her home, moved in with room-mates, and began praying. A lot. During what seemed like the endless shrinking of her life, Alice's church had been able to support her as she moved into austerity mode, along with offering friendship and prayer. This was good and important.

What I want to highlight in this section, though, is what happened next. In all her suffering and confusion, and as she edged in and out of depression, members of her church discerned something that Alice herself could not. In Alice's words,

> Through the discernment process of paying off my home, God un-covered my financial abilities to the church. Only months later the church leadership asked me to head up the benevolence committee. I felt weak and worn down from living seven years with chronic fatigue syndrome. I perceived myself as disabled, but the leadership stressed that I was a pillar of strength, and a valued member of the congre-gation. The invitation to serve gave me the opportunity to focus on something outside myself that encompassed many of my strengths. The words of Jesus to Simon felt true of me, too, "Simon, Simon, behold, Satan demanded to have you, that he might sift you like wheat, but I have prayed for you that your faith may not fail. And when you have turned again, strengthen your brothers." (Lk. 21:31–32) Here was my opportunity to do the same. While serving, my committee members helped me learn to integrate the unpredictable nature of my health issues into a team setting. The benevolence committee was the

precursor, a dry run for initiating the ministry God had for me, which he would unveil six years later.[22]

Alice's church saw that they needed her in a very practical way, when Alice could not see how she could be of any use to them. They saw her creational gifts, and they also saw the Spirit's leading Alice into a new life path. They invited her down that path when they asked her to serve her fellow believers in a committee.

They did not just ask for her to give, though. They waited for her by slowing down to take account of her fluctuating health. This is how discernment works in the body of Christ. They saw things in Alice that she did not see in herself, they invited her beyond herself, and they slowed down in order to make her service practically workable. In this negotiation they became a community more capable of finding a rhythm with people who cannot live up to the pace of the usual church meeting. They waited for one another.

The determination to wait for Alice was to bear clear fruit in Alice's life. She discovered that her love for finance, cycling, and Africa converged with her new awareness of the disability experience. The ministry that blossomed six years later was a charity called His Wheels International. The charity Alice founded created a tricycle that could operate on rough terrain and carry a basket of possessions, propelled only by the rider's arms. Alice's charity created a trike designed for Africa, a continent where many people have missing limbs. Such a human-powered vehicle allows those without legs to rejoin society by restoring their power of mobility. A church that discerned Alice's gifts to the local community eventually served the church's global mission, so alleviating the suffering and alienation of disabled people across a whole continent.

Becoming a Community of Respite

Disability very often creates wounded people. We must be very careful to remember that it is not necessarily the disability itself that causes the wounds. But it does place all kinds of pressures on people, who must constantly face all kinds of concerns that they could never previously have imagined: lost ideals, sheer hard labor, and social awkwardness.

Something as simple as the sleep deprivation associated with some disabilities can spiral into truly devastating repercussions, as Emma, a devout Christian, recalls.

Our son has autism, and at the time of our breakup he was not sleeping through the night. After five years of getting up every night, I was completely exhausted. It affected everything. I felt like my limbs were weighed down and my thoughts were pushing their way through molasses. Without exaggeration, everything I did felt like a massive effort and took an unbelievable amount of concentration.

Astoundingly, three days after Mike left, our son suddenly started to sleep through the night. If that wasn't God helping me out, then I don't know what is! There is no way that I would have coped with the divorce on the two to three hours of sleep per night that I had previously been getting.

I realize now that towards the end of our relationship, Mike and I were living very separate lives as I tried to protect his rest on his day off. Today, our son spends much more time with his dad and they have a better relationship than ever. The respite care that I was previously so desperate for now comes when our son spends alternate weekends with his dad. It gives me a chance to catch up on things, or just rest. It hasn't happened the way I wanted, but I try to make the most of a bad situation.[23]

One biblical theme that I left out of chapter 3 is sabbath. On the seventh day, God rests with the first humans. It is good. Christians are called to rest with God in worship. They are also called to craft collective worship as a place where people whose lives are hard the rest of the week can experience a relaxation of those pressures as they rest with God.

Every Christian needs to understand that many people with disabilities end up fracturing the time of those who live with them. Many children with special needs do not sleep well, leading to sleep exhaustion for parents.

This is why, whatever happens at church, carers and family members almost inevitably have to learn to practice sabbath, as Rachel Wright observes. "After several years of spending more energy than we could replenish, we both got to the end of our rope. We stepped back from church and work commitments, and prioritized rest. With the help of my parents we carved out a day in the week as our 'Sabbath', when we created space and spent time with each other. We put aside drawing up medications nine times a day, hoisting, dressing, physiotherapy and constantly caring."[24]

Churches should reckon with the reality that exhausted parents and carers of disabled children will turn up looking for God at church. If they have created a culture of worship that can give such people rest, they will also be prepared to extend sabbath rest to those wrestling with other sorts of disability experiences, even grief.

What most of these different disability experiences share is that those who have come to worship must do so in the face of their own struggles with grief and with anger. Grief, loss, and dreams going up in smoke very often throw people's faith into question. Churches need to be a place where the pressure of life relaxes enough for people to process emotions that do not follow a predictable sequence.

With a little imagination and commitment churches can really shine in such moments. Jason Whitt, a father of a special needs child, openly admits that the initial experience is one of feeling like a tragedy has happened. Parents are grieving lost dreams they had for their child and dreading an unimaginable future. They are often frustrated by the lack of landmarks and difficulties they are just discovering in the world of disability.

> Yet for most families the grief is transformed into an experience of great joy and blessing. Families begin to recognize that they might not have the child they imagined, but the child they have becomes a source of joy and deep love. As they do for any family at our church who has a newborn, church members coordinated and brought over meals twice a week. . . . As important as the meals were, we could have easily slipped back into isolation if that had been the end of our church's outreach to us. Thankfully, a church family that we only knew in passing drew us out. Rachel Craig called us with an open invitation: we were welcome at their house for dinner every Tuesday night—no strings attached. If we needed to eat and run, that was fine. . . . For the next year and a half we spent almost every Tuesday evening at the Craigs' house.[25]

The Whitts' church community recognized that they would be weathering a practically and emotionally difficult journey, and responded to their basic need for physical support (met through bringing food) and also emotional support (met by offering available and low-demand friendship).

It is easy for families like the Whitts to stop coming to church. Their need and confusion and struggle with God can be so disorienting that they feel unable to come to church, which also happened to the Whitts.

> To draw us out of our exile, our children's minister began a group known as Camille's Companions. Each Sunday a volunteer sits with Camille in the narthex so my wife and I can take our son into the service. . . . What was done as a means of meeting one of our needs has transformed how the teenagers and adults in our church perceive those with disabilities. By looking for ways to make a place for Camille and offer community to our family, our church is discovering that Camille offers gifts back to the body.[26]

Jason Whitt has clearly experienced the service offered to his family, and to Camille, as an environment of loving service that allowed him and his wife to experience church as a place of sabbath rest. Parents and caregivers need this break not only to catch their breath but to gain some perspective on where they are, on the shape of their lives after months and years of hard work and often poor sleep.

Churches will need to continue to think creatively about being a community of respite for families with disabled children as they grow up. Parents' and caregivers' need for a break may slowly give way to teenagers' and young adults' need for meaningful relationships beyond their primary caregivers. There are very few places in modern society where there is enough contact between disabled children and the nondisabled for friendships to form. Again, this is an invitation for the church to shine.

Looking after an ailing parent can be as exhausting as dealing with grief or the bad sleep of a child with disabilities, as Jacober discovered as she was drawing her book on theology and disability to its conclusion.

Sitting down to write this conclusion has been surprisingly difficult. Even as I search for the words I get interrupted, repeatedly. The most recent interruption was to go and repair the wheelchair my mom uses every day. Here I am at the end of this work that has been stirring in my soul for well over a decade and I was frustrated at yet another interruption when it was a task that invited me to live the very theology I am advocating here. . . . Of all people, I want for my own mother to feel included and important, as if she is worth every bit of extra effort and that I have enough to give without worrying whether I will run out. And yet, I do struggle. I do get tired. I do become overwhelmed with the seemingly endless tasks that are added to lists of basic caregiving for those in my life with disabilities.[27]

Sometimes the "least of these" who need the most honor in the church will not be obvious. Sometimes, like Jason Whitt, they will be lawyers. A church that has learned to practice discernment, to wash one another's feet, and to share in one another's joys and pains will be one that looks beyond surfaces to see those among them in need of God's sabbath rest.[28]

Becoming a Community of Friends

Relationships of respite in churches depend on several things.

People or families going through the disability experience have to trust the church enough to make themselves vulnerable by sharing their need. Churches need to find ways to open up spaces where this need is clearly welcomed and can be shared comfortably. That can be as simple as not saying, "Let me know if I can help." Much better is to ask if you can do something concrete—for instance, "I'd love to come to hang out for a few hours with your (insert family member who needs oversight) on Saturday afternoon. Would that be okay?"

Churches also need a measure of realism about their resources. Support goals outside the usual Sunday meeting should be kept manageable. The aim is not to do everything but to find ways to serve one another that people can trust. The most important thing is not to say you are going to do something and then not do it, or to blithely assume that you can handle anything without stopping to listen to the details of what needs to be looked after. One parent explained why reliability is nonnegotiable.

> Families need an uncomplicated, easily accessible means of arranging respite care to meet their wants and needs. When a potential pleasure becomes more than it's worth, I give it up. I always measure the event against the complication involved in making it happen. Time off is no relaxation if I spend the entire time worrying if the kids are OK. I can't enjoy myself if I think they are unhappy, and certainly I can't relax if I'm not confident about the reliability of the person watching my children. I think many professionals are under the misconception that time away from the care of rearing a child with a disability is what I need to maintain my sanity. I need much more than time—*I need security that comes from knowing that the person I've left my son with is as capable as I am of providing for his needs. You simply can't relax and enjoy yourself and worry at the same time. It's peace of mind I need—not just time.*[29]

All work of support and respite must take its cues from the people with disabilities and their expressed needs, and it must be sensitive to the family dynamics involved. Such outreach will only be sustained in congregations that have a strong sense of mission and commitment to one another.

As the church binds itself to those traversing the disability experience, it finds church life enriched as these new relationships expand people's grasp of what it means to live out the image of Christ. It is an enrichment that almost inevitably expands beyond Sunday. The gifts and the claim of those with disabilities may well travel out into the week.

Genuine friendships, for instance, can rarely be constrained to church on Sunday. This is especially true given the reality that many adults with special needs spend almost all their time around others with special needs and the professionals who are paid to care for them. Because our society does not give space for free friendships to form, the church is a place where we can form bonds that are a crucial aspect of human flourishing, as Bill Gaventa points out. "None of us become friends with every person we meet. We are not in control. But we can help people 'choose' and make a commitment to get to know a single person and help that person see his or her own gifts and capacity for doing so."[30] Friendships happen. This is good. And friendship is not a one-day-of-the-week affair.

Becoming a Community of Advocates

If churches become places where those with disabilities feel at home, and their families and carers feel supported, and people become friends, this will be a major achievement. Churches should, however, be warned—it might lead to more!

Churches that risk such interdependence may find themselves taking people to doctor's appointments, checking in on people when their parents are out of town, coordinating transportation, or being available in emergencies.

Social scientific studies have repeatedly highlighted that people with disabilities are more likely to die when they get sick, and more likely to live in poverty. They are many times more likely to be victims of physical and sexual violence, as well as psychological abuse and neglect. These are only the most extreme negative outcomes for people who face much less destructive forms of discrimination on a daily basis in a society that is not designed for their flourishing.

Jesus did not come into the world just to save our souls from hell. He came to unmask and resist the forces that destroy human lives and to restore those lives to fullness.

Having people with disabilities in our churches is a divine reminder that church is not just a refuge from the world but an outpost of God's resistance to the forces that prey upon the weak, as Jacober reminds us.

> Consider this: few people would say they are comfortable with a teenager with Down syndrome being raped. Even fewer would be motivated to take action toward prevention. Once they know a teenager with Down syndrome, however, hear her story, and embrace her community, her witness has the potential to change everything. Advocacy for one individual impacts circumstances for all. The advocacy the church is willing to do for one of her own has the power to change the attitudes and values of the community in which it exists. Advocacy can begin before there is a personal connection. It means saying, from the pulpit,

in Bible study, in music, in church policy, in the training of the greeters
at the doors of the church, that all people are welcome and if something
is a barrier, we will work with you to learn how to change.[31]

If we want to use the language of "unreached people groups,"
those living in care homes are very often the most underserved people
group in modern societies. These fields are ripe for harvest.

I once had the privilege of speaking to the large group of pastors
across all of Scandinavia responsible for leading the confirmation and
discipleship classes for teenagers with special needs. I discovered that
not only are the Norwegians go-getters, but they have a great sense
of humor. They were delighted that the government had just signed
into law a bill that made it mandatory for care homes to take their
residents to church if the resident requested it.

This was all the invitation the Norwegian pastors needed. They
were gleefully taking their church buses from care home to care home,
offering to take those living in them to taster sessions in their churches.
Anyone who wanted to come and put their hand in the water in the
font, or hear how the organ and piano work, and to see what it looks
like from the pulpit was joyously bundled off to church. These pastors' desire for fullness of life for people living in care was written
all over their faces. Their joy in each person whom they introduced
to church was obvious. They knew that it could only enrich the body
of Christ in their local churches.

Lynsay Downs is an Episcopal priest in my diocese in Scotland.
She is also autistic. Her church noticed that some of the people in a
local seniors' home had become incapable of participating in group
gatherings and were being left most of the time in their rooms. They
were noticeably losing weight since there were not enough staff to
take the time they needed to feed them.

Members of Lynsay's church in Banchory now go in several times a
week to sit and feed older people with dementia who would otherwise
be wasting away. They think of this work as honoring human beings
our society no longer knows how to honor. They are slowing down
to be with these aging human beings in a world that believes it does
not have the resources to wait for these elders to finish their supper.

This is what it looks like to be a Philip church.

Being Philip Churches

Readers who have made it to the end of this book have earned a new vision of what is at stake for Christians in the human experience of disability. They have learned how to get past the hesitation blues, weaved through the minefield of disability language, and removed barriers to thinking Christianly about disability that are thrown up by some traditional readings of Scripture and Christian doctrine.

As Christians go forward as church to engage those wrestling with the disability experience, it might be helpful to recall a few of the images discussed in these pages to help solidify this new point of view. The most important biblical image to let shape our vision is that of the apostle Philip. "The Spirit told Philip, 'Go to that chariot and stay near it.' Then Philip ran up to the chariot and heard the man reading Isaiah the prophet" (Acts 8:29–30).

The sociological evidence overwhelmingly shows that people with disabilities are not at church on Sundays or indeed on any other day. Christians can be confident that if people with disabilities turn up in their chariots, or with walkers or seeing eye dogs, with carers or in states of mental ill health, the Spirit has brought them.

One of God's bluntest ways of communicating with the church is by bringing new people into it. Anyone who wants to be with us presents a claim on us that is also a promise to expand and enrich our completeness as the body of Christ. They may not already be reading the Scriptures and asking for an explanation. But their mere presence is a clear sign that they seek living water, the waters of Christ that flow through Scripture and his body, the church.

Philip has to run to keep up with the eunuch's chariot. We will most often have to slow down to the pace of those with disabilities. Paul expresses the logic of the desire of such Christian love succinctly: "When you come together, wait for one another" (1 Cor. 11:33, author trans.). Waiting gives the time for relationship to develop. Waiting acknowledges difference in a patient and generous way. Waiting allows new levels of communication to blossom.

Coming into proximity with people we experience as very different from us also means that our inabilities come to light. Recall that the Good Samaritan too came to this moment. He saw that he needed to solicit the expertise of the innkeeper and that this would cost him money. There is no shame in needing to ask people to teach us how to approach the autistic person or the person with cerebral palsy who needs medical oversight to remain with us. There is no shame in asking such a question because Jesus himself showed us that his body will be one whose health is displayed in the honor that it gives to its least honored members. Their sense of belonging is the index of how much of Christ a local church is imaging.

Philip runs to catch up with the eunuch's chariot and happily agrees to climb up and join him on it. This gesture means that, even while sharing the good news of Jesus Christ, he is inevitably beginning to see the world from the eunuch's point of view. In this process he gains a new appreciation of the power and the scope of the Scriptures they read together.

Even if the eunuch was not reading the Bible, could not have read the Bible, Philip would have climbed up to join him. This proximity becomes the space in which the quiet work of the Spirit can begin to be heard, because we confess as Christians that "to each one the manifestation of the Spirit is given for the common good" (1 Cor. 12:7). *To each one.* The body of Christ is diverse and needs its diversity. Diverse voices reveal the fullness and beauty of the whole body, not just the parts we (mistakenly) think are nice to look on.

To begin to see that beauty is to become, perhaps for the first time, the body we were created to be because "God has put the body together, giving greater honor to the parts that lacked it, so that there should be no division in the body, but that its parts should have equal concern for each other. If one part suffers, every part suffers with it; if one part is honored, every part rejoices with it" (1 Cor. 12:24–26). This is the image of Christ. In such love, humans display Christ's image in the world. Praise be to God.

Afterword

I do not have a reputation as an accessible writer. But I care about people with disabilities, so I've given my utmost to write a book that is accessible to a wide variety of lay readers. Disability is an issue that needs to be understood by the whole church—not just by academic theologians or Christians who feel especially called to disability ministries.

Given my aim in this little book, I did not feel that I could do justice to the life that I live with my son Adam.

Adam has Down syndrome and autism. What insight I might have into the disability experience (my finger notwithstanding) I learned in the seventeen years I've had the pleasure to share with Adam.

Readers who want to read more about him—and the difficulties of speaking well and faithfully about someone who cannot speak for themselves—should read the introduction to my scholarly book on disability, *Wondrously Wounded: Theology, Disability, and the Body of Christ.*

Notes

Chapter 1 Nobody with Disabilities in Our Church

1. Hans Reinders, *Receiving the Gift of Friendship: Profound Disability, Theological Anthropology, and Ethics* (Grand Rapids: Eerdmans, 2008), 335.

2. Erik W. Carter reviews all the relevant research on attendance of people with disabilities in churches, mosques, and synagogues in chap. 1 of *Including People with Disabilities in Faith Communities: A Guide for Service Providers, Families, and Congregations* (Baltimore: Brookes, 2007).

3. Bethany McKinney Fox, *Disability and the Way of Jesus: Holistic Healing in the Gospels and the Church*, foreword by John Swinton (Downers Grove, IL: IVP Academic, 2019), 131.

4. Fox, *Disability and the Way of Jesus*, 134.

5. "Disability Pay Gaps in the UK: 2018," UK Office for National Statistics, last updated December 2, 2019, https://www.ons.gov.uk/peoplepopulationandcommunity/healthandsocialcare/disability/articles/disabilitypaygapsintheuk/2018#nearly-one-in-five-of-the-uk-population-aged-16-to-64-years-was-disabled.

6. "Disability Characteristics," United States Census Bureau, 2018, https://data.census.gov/cedsci/table?q=S1810%3A%20DISABILITY%20CHARACTERISTICS&hidePreview=true&tid=ACSST1Y2018.S1810.

7. Eleanor X. Liu, Erik W. Carter, Thomas L. Boehm, Naomi H. Annandale, and Courtney E. Taylor, "In Their Own Words: The Place of Faith in the Lives of Young People with Autism and Intellectual Disability," *Intellectual and Developmental Disabilities* 52, no. 5 (October 2014): 388–404.

8. Melinda Jones Ault, "Participation of Families of Children with Disabilities in Their Faith Communities: A Survey of Parents" (PhD diss., University of Kentucky, 2010), https://search.proquest.com/docview/919088298.

9. Erik W. Carter, "A Place of Belonging: Research at the Intersection of Faith and Disability," *Review and Expositor* 113, no. 2 (2016): 169.

10. Amy E. Jacober, *Redefining Perfect: The Interplay between Theology and Disability*, foreword by Nick Palermo (Eugene, OR: Cascade Books, 2017), 48–49.

11. Harlan Hahn, paraphrased in Stacy Simplican, *The Capacity Contract: Intellectual Disability and the Question of Citizenship* (Minneapolis: University of Minnesota Press, 2015), 119.

. 12. The blind theologian John Hull relates one such experience of involuntary healing of his eyes in *In the Beginning There Was Darkness: A Blind Person's Conversations with the Bible* (London: SPCK, 2001), 36–38.

13. Frances Young, *Arthur's Call: A Journey of Faith in the Face of Severe Learning Disability* (London: SPCK, 2014), 65.

14. Grant Macaskill, *Autism and the Church: Bible, Theology, and Community* (Waco: Baylor University Press, 2019), 73.

15. Young, *Arthur's Call*, 65.

16. Fox, *Disability and the Way of Jesus*, 71.

Chapter 2 Jesus Heals Everyone He Meets

1. Damon Rose, "Pick Up Your Stretcher and Walk," on *Heart and Soul*, BBC World Service, May 22, 2019, radio broadcast, 27:00, https://www.bbc.co.uk/pro grammes/w3csz41y.

2. Candida R. Moss, *Divine Bodies: Resurrecting Perfection in the New Testament and Early Christianity* (New Haven: Yale University Press, 2019), 32–36.

3. Joni Eareckson Tada with Joni's Kids, *I've Got Wheels!*, Word Treasures, 1985.

4. *Joni*, directed by James F. Collier, World Wide Pictures, 1980.

5. First appearing in 1972, A Thief in the Night is an evangelical Christian film series written by Jim Grant and produced by Donald W. Thompson.

6. John Swinton, foreword to Fox, *Disability and the Way of Jesus*, ix.

7. Swinton, foreword to Fox, *Disability and the Way of Jesus*, xi.

8. Young, *Arthur's Call*, 40. Scripture quotation is from Young's book.

9. Hull, *In the Beginning There Was Darkness*, 64.

10. Quoted in Fox, *Disability and the Way of Jesus*, 82.

11. Rebecca F. Spurrier, *The Disabled Church: Human Difference and the Art of Communal Worship* (New York: Fordham University Press, 2019), 16.

12. Macaskill, *Autism and the Church*, 190.

13. Fox, *Disability and the Way of Jesus*, 105.

14. Fox, *Disability and the Way of Jesus*, 48.

15. Fox, Disability and the Way of Jesus, 30–31. George Engel discusses the "folk model" in "The Need for a New Medical Model: A Challenge for Biomedicine," *Science* 196, no. 4286 (April 8, 1977): 129–36.

16. Engel, "Need for a New Medical Model," 319.

17. Andrew Crislip, *From Monastery to Hospital: Christian Monasticism and the Transformation of Healthcare in Late Antiquity* (Ann Arbor: University of Michigan Press, 2005).

18. The parallel versions of this story in Luke 18:35–43 and Matt. 9:27–31 are illuminating. Mark's version is the most developed and thoughtfully placed, suggesting that he wanted to foreground the story of this healing as especially revealing of Jesus's heart as messiah and healer. Mark's punchline is that "he followed Jesus along the road" (10:52). There is also comedy in Mark's account, as those who hush

Bartimaeus suddenly become his best friends. Mark also positions Bartimaeus as the "last ask" before Jesus's triumphal entry, and his story is followed by the vignette of the foolishly selfish request of James and John to sit next to Jesus in his coming kingdom. This placement again reveals Bartimaeus to be more theologically astute and faithful in his discipleship than the official disciples.

Mark thus sets up a parallel between the reactions of those around to the things being requested in the two stories. James and John ask in secret about the kingdom, which they misunderstand, and with their request provoke jealousy from the other disciples. Bartimaeus asks publicly about a kingdom that he understands and is hushed by the official disciples while finally being fully affirmed by Jesus.

Luke's account just calls the man a "blind man" (18:35) and presents Jesus as responding rather more imperiously, "ordering" him to come over and commanding him to see. The emphasis of Luke's account is on the onlookers seeing the miracle and praising God, and it is the version most susceptible to the critique that the blind man has been instrumentalized as an object lesson by Jesus.

All three Gospels emphasize that the blind man cries out "Son of David, have mercy on me!" and that the combination of the messianic title and the call for mercy is one Jesus cannot pass up.

19. Hull, *In the Beginning There Was Darkness*, 44.

20. Fox, *Disability and the Way of Jesus*, 82, 105.

21. Adam Booth, "'A Death Like His': Saul's Privation and Restoration of Sight as Prophetic Formation in Acts 9," *Journal of Disability & Religion* 22, no. 1 (2018): 51. Quoting Louise J. Lawrence, *Sense and Stigma in the Gospels: Depictions of Sensory-Disabled Characters* (Oxford: Oxford University Press, 2013), 44.

22. Hull, *In the Beginning There Was Darkness*, 165.

23. Hull, *In the Beginning There Was Darkness*, 40.

24. Hull, *In the Beginning There Was Darkness*, 43.

25. Hull, *In the Beginning There Was Darkness*, 32, 38.

26. An extended treatment of this theme can be found in Brian Brock, *Wondrously Wounded: Theology, Disability, and the Body of Christ* (Waco: Baylor University Press, 2019), 49–52.

27. For a survey of this wealth of material, see John A. Davies, *Lift Up Your Heads: Nonverbal Communication and Related Body Imagery in the Bible* (Eugene, OR: Pickwick, 2018).

28. Candida R. Moss, "The Man with the Flow of Power: Porous Bodies in Mark 5:25–34," *Journal of Biblical Literature* 129, no. 3 (2010): 516.

29. "4697. splagchnizomai," in *Strong's Exhaustive Concordance of the Bible*, Biblehub.com, https://biblehub.com/greek/4697.htm.

30. Ivan Illich, *Rivers North of the Future: The Testament of Ivan Illich as Told to David Cayley* (Toronto: Anansi, 2005), 222.

31. Macaskill, *Autism and the Church*, 51.

32. Fox, *Disability and the Way of Jesus*, 145–51.

33. Rachel Wright and Tim Wright, *Shattered: God's View through Life's Broken Windows* (Farnham, UK: CWR, 2019), 157–59. *Shattered* is a workbook intended for use in church reflection on and with families of children with complex needs. For more see Rachel Wright's foundation website, Born at the Right Time: https://www.bornattherighttime.com.

Chapter 3 God Chose You Because He Knew You Could Handle It

1. Jason Whitt quoted in William C. Gaventa, *Disability and Spirituality: Recovering Wholeness* (Waco: Baylor University Press, 2018), 148–49.

2. Kate Bowler's *Everything Happens for a Reason: And Other Lies I've Loved* (New York: Random House, 2018) insightfully discusses the problems with various well-meaning words of Christian comfort, usefully summarizing what to say and not to say in two appendixes.

3. Wright and Wright, *Shattered*, 75–76.

4. Jeremy Schipper, "Healing and Silence in the Epilogue of Job," *Word & World* 30, no. 1 (Winter 2010): 22.

5. Deborah Creamer, *Disability and Christian Theology: Embodied Limits and Constructive Possibilities* (Oxford: Oxford University Press, 2009), 93–94.

6. Amos Yong, *The Bible, Disability, and the Church: A New Vision of the People of God* (Grand Rapids: Eerdmans, 2011), 39–40.

7. Yong, *Bible, Disability, and the Church*, 32 (emphasis added).

8. Author's translation.

9. Yong, *Bible, Disability, and the Church*, 34.

10. "A History of the Eye," Stanford.edu, https://web.stanford.edu/class/history13/earlysciencelab/body/eyespages/eye.html.

11. With thanks to Kirsty Jones for showing me the disability themes in this story.

12. Simon Horne, "'Those Who Are Blind See': Some New Testament Uses of Impairment, Inability, and Paradox," in *Human Disability and the Service of God: Reassessing Religious Practice*, ed. Nancy L. Eiesland and Don E. Saliers (Nashville: Abingdon, 1998), 88–101.

13. Hull, *In the Beginning There Was Darkness*, 113.

14. Young, *Arthur's Call*, 112.

15. Fox, *Disability and the Way of Jesus*, 84.

16. Yong, *Bible, Disability, and the Church*, 66–67. I am aware that the reading I have presented draws out one of the latent meanings of this text and can be countered with one drawing out different textual details that cast Peter's words and actions in a more positive light. In certain contexts, that more positive reading would be appropriate to emphasize. In the context of my treatment here, I am drawing out what appear to be clear points of divergence by the disciples from the "best practice" on display in the healings of Jesus. My intention in doing so is to reassure contemporary Christians that they would not be the first ones to fall short in their engagements with people with disabilities—and so they should not be afraid to reach out to those they are not sure they know how best to approach. We will fail, but God does not take our failure all that seriously. With thanks to Adam D. Ayers for his sermon on this passage and his discussion of how the New Testament writers' approach to the Old Testament depends on textual latency. Adam D. Ayers, *Kingdom in Context* (Skyforest, CA: Urban Loft Publishers, 2020), 113–36.

17. Jacober, *Redefining Perfect*, 7.

18. Hull, *In the Beginning There Was Darkness*, 84–91.

19. Yong, *Bible, Disability, and the Church*, 84.

20. Booth, "'A Death Like His,'" 51.

21. Booth, "'A Death Like His,'" 42.

22. This earliest known picture of Jesus is called the Alexamenos graffito, and it was found etched in plaster in first-century Rome. "Alexamenos Graffito," *Bible Odyssey*, 2019, https://www.bibleodyssey.org/en/tools/image-gallery/a/alexamenos-graffito.

23. I discuss the historical evidence for this claim in Brian Brock and Bernd Wannenwetsch, *The Therapy of the Christian Body: A Theological Exposition of Paul's First Letter to the Corinthians*, vol. 2, foreword by Douglas Campbell (Eugene, OR: Cascade Books, 2018), 53–55.

24. The disability implications of this chapter are discussed in more detail in Brock and Wannenwetsch, *Therapy of the Christian Body*, 66–71.

25. Wright and Wright, *Shattered*, 178.

26. John Swinton, *Becoming Friends of Time: Disability, Timefulness, and Gentle Discipleship* (Waco: Baylor University Press, 2018), chaps. 2, 6.

27. Jacober, *Redefining Perfect*, 66.

28. Moss, *Divine Bodies*, 32–36.

Chapter 4 Disability Is a Tragic Effect of the Fall

1. Benjamin T. Conner, *Disabling Mission, Enabling Witness: Exploring Missiology through the Lens of Disability Studies* (Downers Grove, IL: IVP Academic, 2018), 6.

2. Fox, *Disability and the Way of Jesus*, 185–86.

3. Fox, *Disability and the Way of Jesus*, 186.

4. Nancy L. Eiesland, *The Disabled God: Toward a Liberatory Theology of Disability* (Nashville: Abingdon, 1994), 75.

5. Jacober, *Redefining Perfect*, 28–29.

6. Dietrich Bonhoeffer, "Sermon for Evening Worship Service on 2 Corinthians 12:9, London 1934(?)," in *Berlin, 1933–1935*, Dietrich Bonhoeffer Works 13, ed. Keith W. Clements, trans. Isabel Best (Minneapolis: Augsburg Fortress, 2007), 401.

7. Dietrich Bonhoeffer to Julie Bonhoeffer, Bethel, August 20, 1933, in *Berlin: 1932–1933*, Dietrich Bonhoeffer Works 12, ed. Larry L. Rasmussen, trans. Isabel Best, David Higgins, and Douglas W. Stott (Minneapolis: Augsburg Fortress, 2009), 156–59.

8. Bonhoeffer's experiences at Bethel are recounted in detail in Bernd Wannenwetsch, "'My Strength Is Made Perfect in Weakness': Bonhoeffer and the War over Disabled Life," in *Disability in the Christian Tradition: A Reader*, ed. Brian Brock and John Swinton (Grand Rapids: Eerdmans, 2012), 353–68.

9. Wright and Wright, *Shattered*, 83–84.

10. Wright and Wright, *Shattered*, 141.

11. Hannah Goodliff quoted in Wright and Wright, *Shattered*, 109–10.

12. *Home of Mephibosheth*, directed by Guang Li, produced by Zhongshi Chen (China, 2017).

13. *Home of Mephibosheth*. This movie is the best depiction I know of the practice of Christian love for outcasts that was characteristic of Christians in the first centuries after Christ. To learn more about this important but largely forgotten early Christian history see Brock, *Wondrously Wounded*, 31–35.

14. Paul Murray, "What Hope Is," in *Scars: Essays, Poems and Meditations on Affliction* (London: Bloomsbury, 2014), 92.

15. Stanley Hauerwas, *Dispatches from the Front: Theological Engagements with the Secular* (Durham, NC: Duke University Press, 1994), 183–84. I have replaced

the language of "mentally handicapped" with "learning-impaired people" in this quotation.

16. Jacober, *Redefining Perfect*, 55.

17. Jacober, *Redefining Perfect*, 71–72.

18. Jacober, *Redefining Perfect*, 70.

19. Hull, *In the Beginning There Was Darkness*, 72.

20. Michael J. Buckley, "Because Beset by Weakness . . . ," The Roman Catholic Archdiocese of Atlanta, 1971, 1, http://atlantadiaconateformation.com/weakenough .pdf.

21. Livy, *Historia*, 2.32.9–12, translated in James G. Dunn, *The Theology of Paul the Apostle* (Grand Rapids: Eerdmans, 1998), 550n103.

22. This story is recounted in Don Wood, "*This* Ability: Barth on the Concrete Freedom of Human Life," in Brock and Swinton, *Disability in the Christian Tradition*, 392–93.

23. Wright and Wright, *Shattered*, 64–65.

24. Moss, *Divine Bodies*, chap. 3.

25. Augustine, *The City of God against the Pagans*, ed. and trans. R. W. Dyson (Cambridge: Cambridge University Press, 1998), 22.14.

26. This section summarizes Moss, *Divine Bodies*, chap. 1.

27. I am discussing here Moss, *Divine Bodies*, chap. 3, and Augustine, *City of God*, 22.19.

Chapter 5 We Don't Know Where to Start

1. Conner, *Disabling Mission, Enabling Witness*, 2–3.

2. Conner, *Disabling Mission, Enabling Witness*, 3.

3. I learned this term from Joe Landis, who uses it in the foreword to Dean Preheim-Bartel, Timothy J. Burkholder, Linda A. Christophel, and Christine J. Guth, *Circles of Love: Stories of Congregations Caring for People with Disabilities and Their Families* (Harrisonburg, VA: Herald, 2015), 12.

4. Quoted in Fox, *Disability and the Way of Jesus*, 43–44.

5. Fox, *Disability and the Way of Jesus*, 187.

6. Fox, *Disability and the Way of Jesus*, 188.

7. Benjamin T. Conner, *Amplifying Our Witness: Giving Voice to Adolescents with Developmental Disabilities* (Grand Rapids: Eerdmans, 2012), 32.

8. Jacober, *Redefining Perfect*, 68.

9. Jacober, *Redefining Perfect*, 35.

10. This story is told by a deacon at Sacred Family and quoted in Spurrier, *Disabled Church*, 87.

11. Spurrier, *Disabled Church*, 87.

12. Rachel in Wright and Wright, *Shattered*, 56.

13. Preheim-Bartel et al., *Circles of Love*, 12.

14. Tim in Wright and Wright, *Shattered*, 112–13.

15. Erik Carter usefully draws together the aims of welcome, which are presented in this article: Marianne Holman Prescott, "10 Simple Ways to Create a Sense of Belonging for Children and Adults with Disabilities," Church News, updated February 9, 2018, https://www.thechurchnews.com/living-faith/2018-09-27/ten-simple-ways -to-create-a-sense-of-belonging-for-children-and-adults-with-disabilities-8263.

16. Jacober, *Redefining Perfect*, 32.

17. Jacober, *Redefining Perfect*, 32.

18. Jacober, *Redefining Perfect*, 32–33.

19. Spurrier, *Disabled Church*, 31.

20. Gaventa, *Disability and Spirituality*, 234.

21. Spurrier, *Disabled Church*, 34.

22. Alice Teisan, *Riding on Faith: Keeping Your Balance When the Wheels Fall Off* (self-pub., 2012), 54–55.

23. Quoted in Wright and Wright, *Shattered*, 48–49.

24. Wright and Wright, *Shattered*, 116.

25. Whitt quoted in Gaventa, *Disability and Spirituality*, 149.

26. Whitt quoted in Gaventa, *Disability and Spirituality*, 151.

27. Jacober, *Redefining Perfect*, 101.

28. Here churches inspired to make a start in being a community of respite might take inspiration from parachurch organizations such as The Elisha Foundation, Young Life Capernaum, and Reality Ministries (all have well-developed websites).

29. Quoted in Gaventa, *Disability and Spirituality*, 162 (emphasis original).

30. Gaventa, *Disability and Spirituality*, 227.

31. Jacober, *Redefining Perfect*, 58.

Scripture Index

Subject Index

179

CPSIA information can be obtained
at www.ICGtesting.com
Printed in the USA
LVHW082308300421
686099LV00002B/209